Water Security and the Sustainable Development Goals: Advancing Clean Water Access, Poverty Reduction, Public Health, Gender Equality, Sustainable Agriculture, and Climate Resilience Globally

AF706068

Copyright

Water Security and the Sustainable Development Goals: Advancing Clean Water Access, Poverty Reduction, Public Health, Gender Equality, Sustainable Agriculture, and Climate Resilience

The author and publisher are of the same opinion regarding the views and content expressed in this work.

Disclaimer: The information in this book is provided for general knowledge and educational purposes only. While every effort has been made to ensure accuracy, the author and publisher make no representations or warranties with respect to the completeness or suitability of the content. The author and publisher accept no liability for any errors, omissions, or outcomes resulting from the application of information contained herein. Readers are advised to consult appropriate professionals or authorities before acting on any material presented.

ISBN (eBook): 978-1-991370-92-1

ISBN (Paperback): 978-1-991370-93-8

Published by Our Future Water

First Edition, 2025

Cover design and interior layout by Our Future Water

Table of Contents

Introduction

Water security is a cornerstone of sustainable development, serving as both a dedicated objective and a critical enabler for progress across the entire spectrum of the United Nations Sustainable Development Goals (SDGs). It encompasses the reliable availability of water in sufficient quantity and quality to sustain human health, livelihoods, ecosystems, and production, along with the resilience to withstand and recover from water-related shocks and stresses. Achieving water security is essential not only for meeting basic human needs but also for fostering economic prosperity, environmental sustainability, and social stability.

The 2030 Agenda for Sustainable Development underscores this significance through SDG 6: Clean Water and Sanitation, which sets explicit targets for universal access to safe and affordable drinking water, adequate sanitation, improved water quality, increased water-use efficiency, and the protection and restoration of water-related ecosystems. Yet water security is not confined to SDG 6—it is deeply interconnected with nearly every other goal. From reducing poverty (SDG 1) and improving health and well-being (SDG 3), to promoting gender equality (SDG 5), ensuring food security (SDG 2), expanding access to clean energy (SDG 7), building sustainable cities (SDG 11), and addressing climate change (SDG 13), water is a vital link that binds the SDG framework together.

Despite this centrality, global water systems are under mounting pressure. Climate change is altering precipitation patterns, intensifying droughts and floods, and threatening water quality. Population growth and rapid urbanization are increasing demand, placing unprecedented strain on infrastructure and governance systems. Industrialization, agricultural expansion, and shifts in consumption patterns have heightened competition for finite water resources, often leading to over-extraction, pollution, and environmental degradation. These challenges are compounded by governance gaps, inadequate financing, and inequitable access, which exacerbate vulnerabilities in communities and ecosystems alike.

Addressing these complex and interlinked issues requires an integrated, cross-sectoral approach to water management—one that balances human needs, economic development, and environmental sustainability. This involves recognising the multiple values of water, improving governance and institutional capacity, investing in resilient infrastructure, and promoting cooperation across boundaries and sectors. Effective solutions must also account for the diverse social, economic, and ecological contexts in which water is managed, ensuring that policies and practices are equitable, inclusive, and responsive to the needs of all stakeholders.

This book provides a comprehensive exploration of how water security intersects with, supports, and is supported by each of the SDGs. Through a typological and systemic lens, it examines the multidimensional role of water in achieving sustainable development, highlighting the synergies, trade-offs, and co-benefits that arise from integrated approaches. Each chapter focuses on a specific subset of SDGs, unpacking the pathways through which water security can drive progress and resilience.

Ultimately, this work aims to equip decision-makers, practitioners, and researchers with the knowledge and strategic insight needed to position water as a central pillar of sustainable development. By aligning water security strategies with the SDGs, societies can not only safeguard this essential resource but also unlock transformative opportunities for a more equitable, resilient, and sustainable future.

Chapter 1: Understanding Water Security in the SDG Era

Water security has emerged as a defining challenge and opportunity in the pursuit of the SDGs. It encompasses the reliable availability of adequate quantities and quality of water to sustain livelihoods, human well-being, and socio-economic development, while preserving ecosystems and managing water-related risks. In the SDG era, water security is recognized not only as a standalone objective under SDG 6—ensuring availability and sustainable management of water and sanitation for all—but also as a critical enabler for achieving interconnected goals on poverty reduction, food security, energy, health, gender equality, and climate resilience. Addressing water security requires a holistic perspective that integrates social, economic, and environmental dimensions, balancing competing demands and safeguarding resources for future generations. This chapter explores the evolving concept of water security within the SDG framework, highlighting its centrality to sustainable development and the need for coordinated, inclusive, and adaptive approaches.

Defining Water Security: Availability, Access, Quality, and Sustainability

Water security is a comprehensive concept that goes beyond mere access to water. It integrates the dimensions of availability, access, quality, and sustainability, each of which is essential for ensuring that water resources meet the needs of people, economies, and ecosystems both now and in the future.

Availability refers to the physical presence of sufficient water resources to meet demand. This encompasses surface water, groundwater, and alternative sources such as desalination and treated wastewater. Availability is influenced by natural hydrological cycles, climate variability, and long-term climate change, as well as human activities that alter water distribution, such as land-use change, dam construction, and irrigation expansion. An adequate and reliable supply is the foundation upon which all other aspects of water security are built.

Access is about ensuring that individuals, communities, and economic sectors can obtain water when and where they need it, without discrimination or undue burden. It is shaped by infrastructure development, governance arrangements, and socio-economic factors. Even in regions with abundant water resources, inequitable distribution systems, lack of investment in delivery networks, or political marginalization can create pockets of severe water insecurity. Access also entails affordability—water must be provided at a cost that does not compromise people's ability to meet other basic needs.

Quality focuses on the condition of water and its suitability for various uses, including drinking, sanitation, agriculture, industry, and ecosystem health. Contamination from industrial effluents, agricultural runoff, untreated sewage, and naturally occurring pollutants such as arsenic or fluoride can render water unsafe, with profound consequences for public health and productivity. Maintaining high water quality requires robust pollution control measures, effective wastewater management, and regular monitoring to ensure compliance with standards.

Sustainability underpins the long-term viability of water systems. It demands that water withdrawals do not exceed the rate of natural replenishment and that ecosystems dependent on water are maintained in a healthy state. Sustainability also implies resilience—the capacity of water systems to adapt to and recover from shocks such as droughts, floods, infrastructure failures, or socio-political disruptions. This involves integrated water resources management that balances competing demands across sectors and scales, incorporates climate adaptation strategies, and fosters cooperation among stakeholders.

These four dimensions are interdependent. For example, high-quality water that is available in sufficient quantity is of little use if people cannot access it, while widespread access to poor-quality water can create severe public health crises. Similarly, achieving short-term gains in availability or access by over-exploiting resources can undermine long-term sustainability. Effective water security strategies therefore require a holistic approach that addresses all dimensions simultaneously, recognising that improvements in one area often depend on progress in others.

Moreover, water security must be viewed within the broader socio-economic and environmental context. Population growth, economic development, changing consumption patterns, and technological innovation all influence demand and management approaches. Climate change introduces additional uncertainties, making flexible, adaptive governance essential. By framing water security through the lenses of availability, access, quality, and sustainability, policymakers and practitioners can better identify priorities, allocate resources efficiently, and design interventions that produce lasting, equitable benefits.

Evolution of the Concept Within Global Development Discourse

The concept of water security has evolved significantly over the past several decades, reflecting shifts in global priorities, environmental realities, and development thinking. Initially, water was primarily viewed through the lens of resource supply and infrastructure development, with an emphasis on meeting growing demand through the expansion of reservoirs, irrigation networks, and distribution systems. This supply-driven perspective dominated much of the mid-20th century, aligning with post-war development agendas that prioritized economic growth and industrialization.

By the late 20th century, the limitations of purely supply-side approaches became evident. Rapid population growth, urbanization, and industrial expansion began to outpace infrastructure capacity, while environmental degradation and pollution compromised water quality. At the same time, growing awareness of ecological limits prompted a shift toward integrated water resources management (IWRM), which sought to balance human needs with environmental sustainability. The Dublin Principles of 1992 and the outcomes of the United Nations Conference on Environment and Development (UNCED) in Rio de Janeiro reinforced the idea that water should be managed as an economic good, a social necessity, and an ecological resource.

In the early 2000s, the concept of water security gained traction as a broader framework for understanding water-related risks and opportunities. Influenced by emerging research on climate change and globalization, water security began to encompass issues of governance, resilience, and equity. It moved beyond infrastructure provision to include considerations of vulnerability, adaptive capacity, and cross-sectoral linkages with health, food security, and energy systems. International organizations, including the United Nations and the World Bank, began incorporating water security into strategic development agendas, linking it explicitly to poverty reduction, economic growth, and conflict prevention.

The adoption of the 2030 Agenda for Sustainable Development in 2015 further solidified water security's role within global development discourse. SDG 6, dedicated to clean water and sanitation, framed water security as both a standalone objective and a driver of progress across multiple SDGs. The agenda's emphasis on universality, integration, and inclusivity encouraged a holistic understanding of water security, one that recognizes interdependencies between sectors and the need for coordinated, cross-border action.

Today, water security is understood not only as a technical or environmental challenge but also as a governance, social justice, and geopolitical issue. It is embedded within debates on climate resilience, sustainable urbanization, and global health, making it a central pillar of international cooperation and sustainable development policy. This evolution reflects an increasing recognition that securing water for people, economies, and ecosystems is fundamental to achieving a stable, prosperous, and equitable world.

SDG 6 as the Cornerstone: Targets and Indicators for Water and Sanitation

Sustainable Development Goal 6 (SDG 6) is dedicated to ensuring the availability and sustainable management of water and sanitation for all. It serves as the cornerstone of global efforts to achieve water security, embedding clear targets and indicators that guide action and measure progress. By setting an integrated agenda for water, sanitation, hygiene, and ecosystem protection, SDG 6 provides a framework for countries to align national strategies with global commitments, while fostering accountability and cross-sectoral collaboration.

SDG 6 contains eight targets, six of which focus on outcomes and two on the means of implementation. The outcome targets include achieving universal and equitable access to safe and affordable drinking water (6.1), achieving access to adequate and equitable sanitation and hygiene for all while ending open defecation (6.2), improving water quality through pollution reduction and wastewater treatment (6.3), increasing water-use efficiency and ensuring sustainable withdrawals to address scarcity (6.4), implementing integrated water resources management at all levels (6.5), and protecting and restoring water-related ecosystems (6.6). These targets acknowledge that water security extends beyond supply and access, encompassing quality, sustainability, and governance dimensions.

The two means-of-implementation targets—expanding international cooperation and capacity-building (6.a) and supporting community participation in water and sanitation management (6.b)—reinforce the role of partnerships, finance, and local engagement in delivering the SDG 6 agenda. By integrating capacity development and stakeholder participation, these targets ensure that progress is not just measured in infrastructure terms but also in strengthened institutions and empowered communities.

A robust set of indicators underpins SDG 6, enabling the monitoring of progress and identifying gaps. For example, indicators such as the proportion of the population using safely managed drinking water services and sanitation services track basic service delivery, while metrics on ambient water quality, efficiency in water use, and the extent of IWRM implementation provide insight into sustainability and governance performance. Ecosystem health indicators, such as changes in the extent of water-related ecosystems over time, highlight the environmental dimension of water security.

Importantly, SDG 6 is deeply interconnected with other SDGs. Progress on clean water and sanitation drives improvements in health (SDG 3), education (SDG 4), gender equality (SDG 5), food security (SDG 2), energy access (SDG 7), and sustainable cities (SDG 11). Conversely, advances in these areas reinforce water security by reducing demand pressures, minimizing pollution, and supporting more efficient and equitable resource use. This interdependence underlines the need for integrated policy approaches that cut across sectors.

As the 2030 deadline approaches, achieving SDG 6 requires accelerated action in several areas: expanding investment in infrastructure and services, strengthening governance and institutional capacity, addressing inequalities in access, and safeguarding ecosystems. Without progress on SDG 6, many other SDGs risk falling out of reach. Its role as the cornerstone of water security and sustainable development makes it a critical priority for governments, development partners, and communities alike.

Cross-Sectoral Importance of Water Across the SDG Framework

Water is a fundamental enabler of sustainable development, influencing outcomes across nearly all SDGs. Its cross-sectoral nature means that progress in water management yields wide-ranging benefits, while shortcomings can undermine advances in health, education, economic growth, climate resilience, and environmental protection. Recognising and leveraging these interlinkages is essential for integrated policy and investment strategies that maximize co-benefits and minimize trade-offs.

In the context of poverty reduction (SDG 1), secure access to water supports livelihoods, particularly in agriculture, which is the primary source of income for many low-income households. Inadequate water access, by contrast, can entrench poverty through reduced productivity, increased vulnerability to shocks, and higher costs for basic needs. For health and well-being (SDG 3), safe water and adequate sanitation prevent the spread of waterborne diseases, reduce healthcare costs, and improve quality of life. In education (SDG 4) and gender equality (SDG 5), access to nearby, safe water sources reduces the time burden of water collection, allowing more girls and women to attend school and participate in economic and civic life.

Water's role in food security (SDG 2) and energy (SDG 7) underscores the water–energy–food nexus. Irrigation is critical for agricultural productivity, while energy generation—whether hydropower, thermal power, or renewable technologies—relies on water. Inefficient use or mismanagement in one sector can have cascading effects on the others, emphasizing the need for coordinated resource governance. In economic growth and employment (SDG 8), water-intensive industries such as manufacturing, textiles, and tourism depend on secure and sustainable water supplies, while water-related infrastructure projects create jobs and stimulate investment.

Urban development (SDG 11) is another area where water plays a decisive role. Water-sensitive urban design can reduce flood risk, enhance climate resilience, and improve livability, while wastewater reuse can extend supplies for non-potable purposes. Similarly, climate action (SDG 13) relies heavily on water management strategies, as climate change manifests most directly through shifts in water availability, quality, and distribution. Nature-based solutions and resilient water infrastructure are key adaptation measures.

The environmental dimensions of water security also connect to SDG 14 (Life Below Water) and SDG 15 (Life on Land). Healthy freshwater systems maintain biodiversity, regulate ecosystems, and provide essential services such as nutrient cycling and flood regulation. Degradation of these systems can disrupt entire ecological networks and diminish their capacity to support human and environmental health.

Finally, partnerships for the goals (SDG 17) are vital in addressing water challenges that transcend national boundaries and sectors. Transboundary rivers, shared aquifers, and global water-related crises require international cooperation, data sharing, and joint investments in solutions.

The cross-sectoral importance of water within the SDG framework reinforces the need for integrated, multi-level governance and planning. By embedding water considerations into decision-making across sectors, countries can accelerate progress toward the SDGs, ensure the resilience of development gains, and build a more equitable and sustainable future.

Institutional and Governance Dimensions of Achieving Water Security

Achieving water security requires more than physical infrastructure and technological solutions; it depends fundamentally on the strength and effectiveness of institutional and governance systems. These systems determine how water resources are allocated, managed, and protected, as well as how disputes are resolved and long-term sustainability is ensured. Without sound governance, even well-resourced water systems risk inefficiency, inequity, and environmental degradation.

Institutions—ranging from national ministries and regulatory agencies to local water boards and community organizations—play a central role in coordinating water policy, implementing regulations, and managing day-to-day operations. Effective institutions must have clear mandates, sufficient capacity, and adequate resources to perform their functions. They also need the authority to enforce regulations, monitor compliance, and adapt management practices to changing circumstances such as climate variability or population growth.

Good governance in water security is characterized by transparency, accountability, participation, and equity. Transparency ensures that decisions about water allocation, pricing, and infrastructure investments are made openly, with accessible information for all stakeholders. Accountability requires mechanisms for evaluating performance, addressing grievances, and ensuring that public officials and service providers are held responsible for outcomes. Participation allows for the inclusion of diverse perspectives, particularly those of marginalized groups, in decision-making processes. Equity ensures that all people have fair access to water resources, services, and benefits, regardless of socio-economic status or geographic location.

Integrated Water Resources Management (IWRM) provides a governance framework that promotes coordinated decision-making across sectors and scales. It encourages collaboration among agricultural, industrial, energy, and environmental stakeholders to optimize resource use and minimize conflicts. IWRM also fosters adaptive management, enabling policies to evolve in response to new data, shifting priorities, and emerging risks.

At the transboundary level, governance challenges become more complex. Shared rivers, lakes, and aquifers require cooperative agreements and joint management institutions to prevent disputes and promote equitable sharing. International conventions, such as the UN Watercourses Convention, provide legal frameworks for collaboration, but success often depends on political will, trust-building, and mutual benefit.

Financing and resource mobilization are also critical governance considerations. Sustainable water management requires stable funding sources for infrastructure maintenance, capacity-building, and innovation. Public–private partnerships can help bridge funding gaps, but they must be structured to safeguard public interests and maintain service quality.

Ultimately, achieving water security through robust institutional and governance frameworks demands a balance between centralized oversight and decentralized action. National governments set strategic priorities and regulatory standards, while local institutions implement context-specific solutions and engage directly with communities. This multi-level approach enables governance systems to be both coherent at the national scale and responsive to local needs.

Strong institutions and effective governance are the enabling conditions that transform technical potential into real-world outcomes. By fostering coordination, trust, and inclusivity, governance systems ensure that water security is sustained over time, contributing to broader development goals and resilience in the face of future challenges.

Chapter 2: Water Security and Ending Poverty (SDG 1)

Water security plays a pivotal role in eradicating poverty, as reliable access to safe, affordable, and sustainable water underpins livelihoods, health, and economic opportunity. In the context of SDG 1, which calls for ending poverty in all its forms everywhere, water security is both a foundation and a catalyst for change. Poverty is multidimensional, encompassing deprivations in income, health, education, and living standards—all of which are directly or indirectly influenced by water availability, quality, and management. Communities lacking secure water supplies are more vulnerable to economic shocks, disease outbreaks, and environmental hazards, perpetuating cycles of deprivation. Conversely, investments in water infrastructure, governance, and equitable service provision can unlock pathways to income generation, improved well-being, and resilience. This chapter examines how strengthening water security contributes to poverty alleviation, exploring the interconnections between water access, vulnerability reduction, livelihoods, and inclusive economic growth.

The Role of Water Access in Reducing Multidimensional Poverty

Access to safe, reliable, and affordable water is a fundamental determinant of human well-being and a key driver in reducing multidimensional poverty. Unlike income-based poverty measures, multidimensional poverty captures deprivations across several dimensions, including health, education, and living standards. Water access plays a central role in addressing each of these dimensions, making it a powerful lever for holistic poverty alleviation.

In the health dimension, secure water access directly reduces the incidence of waterborne diseases such as cholera, diarrhea, and dysentery, which disproportionately affect low-income communities. Poor health not only diminishes quality of life but also limits the ability to work, attend school, and engage productively in society. Reliable water access also supports better hygiene and sanitation, breaking transmission pathways for many preventable illnesses and reducing the burden on often overstretched healthcare systems.

From an education perspective, lack of water access often translates into reduced school attendance, especially for girls, who are more likely to be tasked with water collection. Long daily trips to fetch water can consume hours, leaving little time for schooling and homework. The absence of safe sanitation facilities in schools further discourages attendance, particularly during menstruation. By reducing the time and physical effort required to obtain water and ensuring proper sanitation, communities can improve school participation rates, educational attainment, and ultimately human capital development.

In terms of livelihoods and income generation, water is essential for agricultural productivity, livestock management, and small-scale industry—all of which are common sources of income in rural and peri-urban areas. Without reliable water, crop yields and livestock health suffer, reducing household income and food security. In urban contexts, access to water can be the difference between viable and unviable small businesses, such as food preparation, laundry services, and manufacturing. Thus, improving water access can boost economic opportunities and provide a pathway out of poverty.

Water access also has a multiplier effect on time poverty. In many low-income settings, households—often women and children—spend substantial amounts of time collecting water from distant or unsafe sources. This time burden limits opportunities for education, paid work, and participation in community life. By ensuring water is available close to homes and workplaces, communities can reclaim time for productive, educational, and leisure activities, contributing to overall well-being.

Equity considerations are also central. Marginalized groups, including those in remote areas, informal settlements, and conflict-affected regions, often face the greatest barriers to water access. Addressing these disparities is critical for ensuring that poverty reduction efforts are inclusive and that no one is left behind. Policy interventions must therefore priorities underserved areas and incorporate community participation to ensure that solutions are culturally appropriate and sustainable.

Finally, water access underpins resilience against shocks. Communities with secure water supplies are better able to cope with droughts, floods, economic downturns, and public health crises. For instance, during the COVID-19 pandemic, access to water for handwashing became a frontline defense against disease spread, underscoring its role in both immediate and long-term resilience.

In sum, improving water access is not just about meeting a basic human need—it is a strategic investment in human development. By reducing disease, freeing time, enabling education, supporting livelihoods, and enhancing resilience, water access directly addresses the multiple deprivations that constitute multidimensional poverty. As such, it should be at the center of integrated poverty alleviation strategies, supported by robust infrastructure, effective governance, and sustainable resource management.

Economic Vulnerability and Water-Related Shocks (Floods, Droughts)

Water-related shocks, such as floods and droughts, are among the most significant natural hazards affecting economies worldwide. They can cause extensive damage to infrastructure, disrupt livelihoods, and undermine economic stability, particularly in countries and communities with limited adaptive capacity. The impacts are often long-lasting, compounding existing vulnerabilities and hindering progress toward sustainable development.

Floods pose immediate and severe threats to economic systems. They damage homes, transport networks, energy infrastructure, and water supply systems, often requiring costly repairs and reconstruction. Floodwaters can also destroy crops, reduce agricultural productivity, and disrupt market access, leading to food shortages and price volatility. In urban areas, flooding can halt industrial production, close businesses, and cause significant losses in the service sector. For low-income households and small enterprises, recovery can be slow due to limited access to insurance, credit, or government support, deepening cycles of poverty.

Droughts, by contrast, exert more gradual but equally devastating effects. Reduced water availability constrains agricultural output, leading to crop failures, livestock deaths, and declining incomes for farming communities. Industries dependent on large volumes of water—such as manufacturing, textiles, and energy production—face operational slowdowns or shutdowns, resulting in job losses and reduced economic output. Prolonged droughts also strain public water utilities, increasing costs for water sourcing, treatment, and distribution. These pressures can drive up water prices, further burdening households and businesses.

Both floods and droughts disrupt trade and supply chains. Flooded transport corridors or drought-reduced hydropower generation can limit the movement of goods and energy, affecting both domestic and export markets. In regions dependent on agriculture, shocks to water availability can undermine export earnings, weaken national balance sheets, and trigger inflationary pressures. Such economic instability can erode investor confidence and limit the fiscal space available for recovery and resilience-building.

Vulnerability to water-related shocks is often higher in areas with inadequate infrastructure, weak governance, and insufficient early warning systems. Informal settlements in flood-prone zones, for example, may lack drainage systems, increasing both the frequency and severity of flood impacts. Rural communities without secure irrigation or drought-resistant crops are highly susceptible to water scarcity. Governance gaps can delay disaster response, while poor land-use planning can exacerbate hazard exposure.

Strengthening resilience to these shocks requires a combination of structural and non-structural measures. Infrastructure investments, such as flood defenses, stormwater management systems, and drought-resilient irrigation schemes, can reduce direct impacts. Early warning systems and climate-informed planning enable timely responses, while economic diversification reduces dependence on climate-sensitive sectors. Financial instruments, such as weather-indexed insurance and emergency funds, provide a safety net for affected populations and businesses.

Ultimately, addressing the economic vulnerability caused by water-related shocks demands an integrated approach that combines risk reduction, adaptive management, and sustainable water governance. By reducing exposure, enhancing adaptive capacity, and promoting equitable recovery, societies can minimize the long-term economic costs of floods and droughts, safeguarding livelihoods and supporting resilient, inclusive growth.

Livelihoods, Agriculture, and Rural Water Systems

Water is a cornerstone of rural livelihoods, particularly in communities where agriculture is the dominant economic activity. Reliable access to water supports crop cultivation, livestock rearing, aquaculture, and a range of small-scale industries, forming the foundation of food security and income generation. In many rural areas, water resources are not only essential for economic survival but also deeply intertwined with cultural practices and community identity.

Agriculture remains the largest consumer of freshwater globally, accounting for about 70% of withdrawals. In rural economies, this reliance is even greater, making water availability a key determinant of productivity and resilience. Irrigation systems, whether traditional or modern, can dramatically increase crop yields, enable multiple planting cycles, and allow cultivation of higher-value crops. Conversely, insufficient or unreliable water supplies can lead to low productivity, crop failure, and income loss, perpetuating cycles of poverty. Livestock production is similarly water-dependent, requiring both drinking water and sufficient pastureland sustained by reliable rainfall or irrigation.

Rural water systems serve not only agricultural needs but also domestic requirements for drinking, cooking, hygiene, and sanitation. Integrated rural water management that balances these competing uses is critical to sustaining community health and economic well-being. However, rural water systems often face significant challenges, including inadequate infrastructure, limited maintenance capacity, and vulnerability to climate variability. Droughts, floods, and changing rainfall patterns can disrupt supply, while overuse or contamination of groundwater can compromise long-term sustainability.

In many rural settings, the lack of investment in water infrastructure creates a bottleneck for development. Irrigation channels may be unlined, leading to high water losses, or pumping systems may be inefficient and costly to operate. Inadequate storage capacity means that excess water during wet seasons cannot be preserved for dry periods, forcing reliance on unpredictable rainfall. Addressing these challenges requires targeted investments in resilient infrastructure, efficient technologies such as drip irrigation, and capacity-building for local water management institutions.

Water governance in rural areas is often decentralized, with community-based management playing a central role. While local control can enhance responsiveness and accountability, it also requires strong institutional support, clear rights and responsibilities, and mechanisms for conflict resolution. Equitable water allocation is particularly important in preventing disputes between upstream and downstream users, or between agricultural and domestic needs.

Climate change adds an additional layer of complexity, intensifying water scarcity in some regions while increasing flood risks in others. Adaptation strategies, such as the adoption of drought-resistant crops, diversification of livelihoods, and improved watershed management, are essential to safeguarding both water resources and rural incomes. Integrating climate information into rural water planning can help communities anticipate and prepare for shifting conditions.

Strengthening rural water systems is not only about ensuring agricultural productivity—it is about supporting the entire fabric of rural life. Reliable, well-managed water supplies enhance food security, improve health outcomes, empower women (who often bear responsibility for water collection), and provide a platform for broader economic diversification. By investing in sustainable rural water systems, policymakers and development partners can unlock pathways to resilience, prosperity, and equitable growth in rural communities.

Infrastructure Investment and Pro-Poor Water Strategies

Investing in water infrastructure is essential for expanding access, improving service quality, and building resilience, particularly for marginalized and low-income communities. Infrastructure encompasses a wide range of systems, including water supply networks, treatment plants, storage facilities, and sanitation services. Without adequate investment, these systems cannot meet growing demand or adapt to the pressures of climate change, urbanization, and population growth.

Pro-poor water strategies aim to ensure that infrastructure investment prioritizes the needs of disadvantaged populations. This involves targeting areas with low service coverage, designing systems that are affordable to operate and maintain, and addressing both rural and urban inequalities. Such approaches recognize that market forces alone rarely deliver equitable water access, making public investment and policy intervention critical.

In rural areas, infrastructure investment often focuses on small-scale, decentralized systems such as community-managed boreholes, gravity-fed schemes, and rainwater harvesting facilities. These solutions can be cost-effective and adaptable to local conditions, provided they are supported by training for operation and maintenance. In urban and peri-urban contexts, expanding piped networks, upgrading informal settlement services, and improving wastewater management are key to reducing health risks and enhancing quality of life.

Financing mechanisms are central to the success of pro-poor strategies. Blended finance, combining public funds, concessional loans, and private investment, can help bridge funding gaps. Tariff structures should be designed to ensure affordability for low-income households while maintaining financial sustainability for service providers. Lifeline tariffs, cross-subsidies, and targeted subsidies are common tools for achieving this balance.

Beyond physical infrastructure, investments must strengthen institutional capacity and governance. This includes improving regulatory oversight, enhancing transparency, and fostering community participation in planning and decision-making. When communities are actively involved, infrastructure projects are more likely to reflect local priorities, gain user acceptance, and remain operational over the long term.

Climate resilience is another critical consideration. Infrastructure must be designed to withstand extreme events such as floods and droughts, and to cope with gradual shifts in water availability. Incorporating nature-based solutions, such as wetland restoration or green stormwater systems, can enhance resilience while providing additional environmental benefits.

Effective pro-poor water strategies require integration across sectors. Linking water investments with initiatives in health, education, and economic development can amplify their impact. For example, improved water access in schools can boost attendance rates, while reliable water supply for small businesses can increase income opportunities.

By aligning infrastructure investment with pro-poor principles, governments and development partners can close service gaps, reduce inequalities, and improve the well-being of vulnerable populations. Such investments not only meet immediate needs but also lay the groundwork for sustainable and inclusive growth.

Strengthening Water Governance to Support Poverty Alleviation

Effective water governance is essential for ensuring that water resources contribute to poverty alleviation. Governance encompasses the policies, institutions, and processes through which decisions about water use, allocation, and management are made and implemented. Strong governance frameworks can ensure equitable access, protect resources from overuse and degradation, and promote the sustainable economic benefits that water can provide to low-income communities.

One of the key principles in pro-poor water governance is equity. Decision-making must priorities the needs of marginalized populations, including those living in rural areas, informal urban settlements, and regions prone to water scarcity. Establishing clear water rights and transparent allocation mechanisms can help prevent exclusion and ensure that all groups, particularly the most vulnerable, have access to sufficient and safe water for domestic and productive uses.

Participation is equally important. Engaging communities in the governance process ensures that policies and infrastructure projects reflect local realities and priorities. Community-based water management models, where users are actively involved in planning, operation, and oversight, can foster accountability and improve the long-term sustainability of water systems. Such participatory approaches also help build local capacity, giving communities the skills and knowledge to manage their resources effectively.

Institutional capacity-building is a critical enabler. Water management agencies at all levels need the technical expertise, financial resources, and legal authority to implement regulations, monitor usage, and enforce compliance. This includes developing data and information systems that allow for evidence-based decision-making, as well as creating mechanisms for coordination between different sectors and administrative levels.

Anti-corruption measures play a significant role in strengthening governance. Transparent procurement processes, public disclosure of budgets and project outcomes, and independent audits help ensure that investments in water infrastructure and services benefit intended communities rather than being diverted by inefficiency or misuse of funds.

Linking water governance to broader poverty alleviation strategies can maximize impact. For example, integrating water management with agricultural development programs can increase productivity and incomes, while coupling governance reforms with health and education initiatives can improve well-being and social outcomes. Recognising the interconnections between water security and other development goals encourages policies that deliver multiple benefits.

Finally, adaptive governance is essential in the face of climate change and other evolving challenges. Institutions must be able to respond flexibly to shifting conditions, such as changes in rainfall patterns, population growth, or economic transitions, while maintaining a focus on equity and poverty reduction.

Strengthening water governance to support poverty alleviation requires a coordinated effort between governments, civil society, the private sector, and local communities. When governance systems are transparent, inclusive, and well-resourced, they can transform water from a source of vulnerability into a driver of economic opportunity and resilience for the poorest members of society.

Chapter 3: Ensuring Water for Health and Wellbeing

Access to safe and sufficient water is fundamental to protecting human health and promoting overall wellbeing. Without reliable water services, communities face heightened risks of waterborne diseases, malnutrition, and preventable deaths, undermining progress toward universal health coverage and sustainable development. Water security ensures not only the availability of drinking water but also the provision of adequate sanitation and hygiene, which are critical to preventing disease transmission and maintaining public health systems. The relationship between water and health extends beyond physical illness, as water scarcity and poor quality can also contribute to stress, anxiety, and reduced quality of life. In urban and rural settings alike, resilient water systems support hospitals, clinics, and emergency responses, strengthening the capacity of health systems to cope with both routine needs and crises. This chapter explores how ensuring water for health and wellbeing underpins sustainable development, safeguards communities, and supports human dignity.

Safe Water and Its Link to Disease Prevention

Safe water is fundamental to public health, serving as a frontline defense against a range of communicable diseases. Access to clean and safe water significantly reduces the transmission of waterborne pathogens, prevents outbreaks, and supports overall health and well-being. The relationship between water safety and disease prevention is direct and well-documented, making it one of the most cost-effective public health interventions.

Many of the most prevalent and deadly diseases in low- and middle-income countries are linked to unsafe water. Pathogens such as Vibrio cholerae, Salmonella typhi, and various strains of Escherichia coli are transmitted through contaminated drinking water, leading to illnesses such as cholera, typhoid fever, and diarrheal diseases. These illnesses remain a leading cause of mortality among children under five, underscoring the urgency of ensuring safe water access. Even in higher-income countries, lapses in water safety can result in significant outbreaks, demonstrating that vigilance is required at all levels of development.

Water safety also plays a crucial role in preventing parasitic infections. Schistosomiasis, for example, is spread through freshwater contaminated with parasites carried by snails, while Guinea worm disease is transmitted via larvae in stagnant water. Eliminating these diseases depends on ensuring that communities have access to protected, well-managed water sources and are educated on safe water practices.

The link between safe water and disease prevention extends beyond drinking water to include water for hygiene and sanitation. Without adequate water supplies, handwashing, food preparation, and cleaning are compromised, increasing the risk of fecal–oral transmission of pathogens. The COVID-19 pandemic highlighted the critical importance of water for hygiene, with handwashing promoted globally as a key preventive measure.

Water treatment and protection measures are central to maintaining water safety. This includes source protection to prevent contamination from human and animal waste, industrial pollutants, and agricultural runoff. Treatment processes such as filtration, chlorination, and ultraviolet disinfection ensure that pathogens are removed or inactivated before water reaches consumers. Ongoing monitoring of water quality, coupled with rapid response mechanisms when contamination is detected, is vital to safeguarding public health.

Infrastructure improvements alone are insufficient without effective governance, public awareness, and community engagement. Public health campaigns can promote safe storage and handling of water in households, reducing recontamination risks. Training local water managers in maintenance and monitoring helps sustain safe water systems over the long term.

The health benefits of safe water are far-reaching. Reducing disease burden lowers healthcare costs, increases productivity, and improves school attendance. Healthy populations are better able to contribute to economic growth and community resilience, creating a positive feedback loop between water security and development.

Investing in safe water is one of the most impactful strategies for preventing disease and improving public health outcomes. By integrating water safety into broader health, education, and development policies, governments and partners can achieve significant gains in well-being, reduce preventable deaths, and move closer to achieving global health and sustainable development goals.

Sanitation, Hygiene, and Public Health Systems

Sanitation and hygiene are foundational pillars of public health, directly influencing disease prevention, life expectancy, and quality of life. Adequate sanitation involves the safe management of human waste, including collection, transport, treatment, and disposal. Hygiene encompasses the practices that maintain cleanliness and prevent disease transmission, such as handwashing, food safety, and menstrual hygiene management. When these elements are integrated into robust public health systems, the result is a significant reduction in morbidity and mortality rates.

Poor sanitation is a primary driver of many preventable diseases, including diarrheal illnesses, cholera, typhoid, and intestinal worm infections. Contamination of water sources by untreated wastewater or open defecation allows pathogens to spread rapidly through communities. Inadequate sanitation facilities in healthcare settings can also undermine infection prevention and control, increasing the risk of healthcare-associated infections. Addressing these issues requires both infrastructure investment—such as sewer networks, septic systems, and treatment plants—and behavioral change initiatives to promote consistent and correct sanitation practices.

Hygiene practices are equally critical in breaking transmission pathways for infectious diseases. Regular handwashing with soap significantly reduces the risk of fecal–oral disease transmission and has been proven to cut diarrheal disease incidence by nearly half in some settings. Safe food handling, menstrual hygiene management, and proper household cleaning are additional practices that support overall community health. Ensuring the availability of water, soap, and hygiene facilities in public places, schools, and workplaces is essential for sustaining these behaviors.

Public health systems provide the institutional framework for managing sanitation and hygiene at scale. This includes policy development, regulation, and service delivery, as well as public education campaigns that encourage healthy behaviors. Coordination across sectors—water, health, education, and urban planning—is vital to create an enabling environment where sanitation and hygiene improvements are maintained over time. Surveillance systems that track disease outbreaks and monitor water quality also allow for timely interventions to protect public health.

The integration of sanitation and hygiene into public health strategies has broader socio-economic benefits. Improved sanitation reduces the time and cost burdens on healthcare systems, increases school attendance (particularly for girls), and boosts workforce productivity by reducing illness-related absenteeism. Investments in these areas often yield high returns, both in terms of health outcomes and economic gains.

Climate change and rapid urbanization present new challenges for sanitation and hygiene systems, particularly in informal settlements and disaster-prone areas. Resilient infrastructure, decentralized treatment solutions, and community-led initiatives can help address service gaps in such contexts.

Strengthening the link between sanitation, hygiene, and public health requires a combination of infrastructure, education, governance, and community engagement. When supported by adequate resources and political commitment, these efforts can dramatically improve health outcomes, break cycles of poverty, and contribute to achieving global development goals.

Managing Pollution and Waterborne Disease Risks

Managing pollution and mitigating waterborne disease risks are central to safeguarding public health and achieving water security. Pollution in water sources can originate from multiple pathways, including untreated sewage, industrial discharges, agricultural runoff, and improper waste disposal. When contaminants enter rivers, lakes, groundwater, or coastal waters, they can compromise the safety of drinking water supplies, disrupt ecosystems, and increase the prevalence of diseases.

Waterborne diseases such as cholera, typhoid fever, and hepatitis A are primarily transmitted through the ingestion of water contaminated with human or animal waste. In addition to bacterial and viral pathogens, protozoa such as Giardia and Cryptosporidium can cause severe gastrointestinal illnesses. Outbreaks are more common in regions with inadequate sanitation infrastructure and limited water treatment capacity, but even high-income countries can experience contamination events if safeguards fail.

Effective management begins with preventing pollution at its source. This includes expanding access to adequate sanitation facilities, ensuring proper wastewater collection and treatment, and implementing measures to prevent industrial and agricultural pollutants from entering waterways. For agriculture, best management practices such as buffer strips, controlled fertilizer application, and proper manure storage can reduce nutrient and pathogen runoff. In industrial sectors, stricter effluent standards and enforcement mechanisms are critical for compliance.

Water treatment plays a vital role in breaking disease transmission pathways. Municipal treatment systems typically combine filtration, sedimentation, and disinfection (e.g., chlorination or ultraviolet light) to remove or neutralize pathogens. However, decentralized or household-level solutions—such as point-of-use filters or solar disinfection—are also important in rural or underserved areas. Regular maintenance and monitoring are essential to ensure these systems remain effective over time.

Surveillance and early warning systems are key components of risk management. Continuous water quality monitoring can detect contamination events quickly, enabling prompt interventions such as issuing boil-water advisories, deploying mobile treatment units, or temporarily switching to alternative sources. Public health surveillance, which tracks disease incidence, can help identify patterns and potential outbreaks linked to water quality issues.

Community engagement and education are equally important. Public awareness campaigns can promote safe water storage and handling practices, reducing the risk of recontamination at the household level. Training for local operators and community leaders can improve water system management and encourage compliance with pollution control measures.

Climate change adds complexity to managing pollution and disease risks. Increased frequency of floods can overwhelm sanitation systems and spread contaminants, while droughts can concentrate pollutants in shrinking water supplies. Adaptive strategies, such as designing resilient infrastructure and incorporating nature-based solutions like constructed wetlands, can help mitigate these challenges.

By combining pollution prevention, robust treatment systems, effective surveillance, and community participation, it is possible to significantly reduce waterborne disease risks. These integrated approaches protect public health, enhance ecosystem integrity, and contribute to the long-term sustainability of water resources.

Mental Health and Stress Under Water Scarcity Scenarios

flexibility. Protecting these sources from pollution through watershed management, buffer zones, and strict regulation further enhances resilience.

Infrastructure design and maintenance are equally important. Systems should be built to withstand extreme weather events, including floods and droughts, which are becoming more frequent and severe due to climate change. This may involve elevating key infrastructure in flood-prone areas, reinforcing pipelines, expanding storage capacity, and incorporating backup power supplies for pumping and treatment facilities. Regular maintenance and timely repairs are critical to prevent small issues from escalating into major disruptions.

Effective water treatment and quality monitoring are core components of resilience. Treatment plants must have the capacity to handle variations in raw water quality, while continuous monitoring enables rapid detection of contamination. In emergencies, portable treatment units or decentralized systems can provide safe water until normal operations are restored. Ensuring that healthcare facilities always have access to safe water is particularly important for infection prevention and control.

Governance and institutional capacity underpin system resilience. Clear roles and responsibilities, adequate funding, trained personnel, and strong coordination between water, health, and emergency management agencies enable timely responses to crises. Community involvement in planning and decision-making enhances local ownership and ensures that solutions reflect specific needs and contexts.

Resilience also depends on robust contingency planning. This includes risk assessments, early warning systems, and response protocols for a range of scenarios, from disease outbreaks to infrastructure damage. Regular drills and training exercises help ensure that staff and communities know how to act during an emergency.

Integrating climate adaptation and disaster risk reduction strategies into water system planning ensures long-term sustainability. Nature-based solutions, such as wetland restoration and green infrastructure for stormwater management, can complement engineered systems, providing additional buffers against extreme events.

By prioritizing resilience in water system design, management, and governance, communities can protect public health, reduce vulnerabilities, and enhance their capacity to recover quickly from disruptions. In turn, this strengthens overall health security and supports broader sustainable development objectives.

Chapter 4: Water in Education, Gender Equality, and Equity (SDGs 4 & 5)

Water security plays a pivotal role in advancing education, gender equality, and social equity. In many regions, the absence of safe and accessible water disproportionately affects girls, who are often tasked with water collection, limiting their time for schooling and perpetuating cycles of disadvantage. Inadequate water, sanitation, and hygiene facilities in schools can hinder attendance, particularly for adolescent girls during menstruation, and reduce overall learning outcomes. Equitable access to water and sanitation services creates safer, more inclusive educational environments and reduces gender-based barriers, enabling all students to participate fully in academic life. Beyond education, improving water access and management can shift household responsibilities, empower women in decision-making roles, and strengthen their participation in community development. Addressing water inequalities is therefore essential not only for achieving gender parity but also for building inclusive societies where opportunities and resources are shared fairly among all.

Impact of Water Insecurity on Girls' Education and School Attendance

Water insecurity has far-reaching implications for education, and its effects are particularly acute for girls. In many parts of the world, the burden of water collection falls disproportionately on women and girls, consuming significant amounts of time each day and reducing opportunities for education. This gendered responsibility perpetuates cycles of inequality, limiting girls' access to schooling and diminishing their prospects for economic and social empowerment.

One of the most direct impacts of water insecurity on girls' education is the loss of instructional time. In rural and peri-urban areas without reliable water infrastructure, girls may spend several hours each day walking to and from water sources. This time burden often coincides with school hours, leading to frequent absenteeism or complete withdrawal from school. Even when girls attend, fatigue from long water collection journeys can affect concentration and academic performance.

Water scarcity also affects school attendance through inadequate sanitation facilities. In many schools, the absence of gender-segregated, safe, and hygienic toilets discourages attendance, especially for adolescent girls during menstruation. Without access to water for washing, girls may prefer to stay home during their menstrual periods, missing several days of school each month. Over time, this absenteeism contributes to lower academic achievement and higher dropout rates.

The physical and emotional toll of water insecurity further undermines educational outcomes. Carrying heavy water containers over long distances can cause musculoskeletal injuries and fatigue, affecting girls' overall health. Exposure to unsafe or remote water collection points can also increase the risk of harassment or violence, creating additional psychological stress. Such risks can lead families to priorities safety over education, keeping girls at home.

In some contexts, water scarcity impacts the broader school environment. Schools without reliable water supplies cannot provide drinking water, support hygiene practices, or maintain clean and safe facilities. This not only deters attendance but can also contribute to the spread of waterborne diseases, resulting in illness-related absenteeism among both students and teachers.

Addressing these challenges requires integrated solutions that combine water, sanitation, and education interventions. Investments in community water infrastructure—such as boreholes, piped networks, and rainwater harvesting systems—can reduce the time burden on girls, freeing up hours for study and rest. At the school level, the provision of safe, accessible, and gender-segregated sanitation facilities is critical. Menstrual hygiene management programs, including access to sanitary products and private washing areas, can help ensure that girls do not miss school during their periods.

Community engagement is equally important. Changing social norms around the division of water collection responsibilities can reduce the disproportionate burden on girls. Education campaigns that highlight the importance of girls' schooling, alongside practical measures to improve water access, can shift household priorities in favour of education.

By addressing the root causes of water insecurity and its gendered impacts, policymakers and development partners can create conditions that support equal educational opportunities. Ensuring that girls have the time, health, and safe environments they need to attend school is not only a matter of equity but also a strategic investment in broader social and economic development. Educated girls are more likely to contribute to community well-being, participate in decision-making, and break the intergenerational cycle of poverty, making water security a powerful lever for transformative change.

Gendered Roles in Water Collection and Household Responsibilities

In many societies, the responsibility for water collection and household water management falls disproportionately on women and girls. This gendered division of labor is deeply rooted in cultural norms, economic structures, and traditional roles, and it has significant implications for gender equality, health, education, and livelihoods.

Women are often considered the primary managers of household water, responsible not only for collecting it but also for ensuring its availability for cooking, cleaning, laundry, hygiene, and caring for children, the sick, and the elderly. In rural and peri-urban areas without reliable water infrastructure, this task can require travelling long distances, sometimes multiple times a day, to reach the nearest water source. The time spent on these journeys can consume several hours daily, limiting opportunities for education, paid work, and participation in community or political life.

Girls frequently share or inherit these responsibilities from a young age, often at the expense of their schooling. The need to assist with water collection can lead to absenteeism, reduced study time, or early school dropout. This perpetuates cycles of inequality, as reduced educational attainment limits future economic opportunities and reinforces traditional gender roles.

The physical burden of carrying heavy water containers over long distances poses health risks, including musculoskeletal injuries, fatigue, and complications during pregnancy. Additionally, the task can expose women and girls to safety risks, particularly in remote or isolated areas where they may face harassment, assault, or other forms of violence. These risks can have lasting psychological impacts and contribute to heightened vulnerability.

The gendered nature of water responsibilities also affects decision-making power within households and communities. Even though women are the primary users and managers of household water, they are often excluded from water governance structures and policy discussions. This exclusion limits the integration of their needs and perspectives into water management strategies, potentially leading to solutions that are less effective or sustainable.

Addressing these disparities requires both practical and structural changes. Expanding access to safe, nearby, and reliable water sources can reduce the time and effort required for collection, freeing women and girls to pursue education, employment, and other activities. Integrating women into water governance bodies and decision-making processes ensures that policies and infrastructure investments reflect their priorities and lived experiences. Public awareness campaigns can help challenge gender norms that assign water collection as a female-only responsibility, encouraging more equitable sharing of household duties.

By recognising and addressing the gendered dimensions of water collection and household responsibilities, policymakers and development practitioners can promote gender equality while improving water security. Reducing the disproportionate burden on women and girls not only benefits them directly but also strengthens community resilience, economic productivity, and overall social well-being.

Empowering Women Through Inclusive Water Management

Inclusive water management is a critical pathway for promoting gender equality and empowering women. Given that women are often the primary users, managers, and custodians of water in households and communities, their involvement in water governance and decision-making is essential to ensure that policies and systems meet the needs of all stakeholders.

Historically, women have been underrepresented in formal water governance structures, from local committees to national policymaking bodies. This exclusion has led to water management approaches that may overlook the practical and strategic needs of women, such as the proximity of water points, the safety of access routes, or the importance of water for household-based livelihoods. By bringing women into decision-making processes, water management can become more responsive, equitable, and sustainable.

Empowering women in this context begins with ensuring their meaningful participation, not just token representation. Women need the opportunity to influence priorities, contribute local knowledge, and shape solutions. This requires addressing barriers such as limited access to education and training, cultural norms restricting women's leadership roles, and time constraints caused by disproportionate domestic responsibilities. Capacity-building programs can equip women with technical skills in water resource management, financial management, and governance, enhancing their confidence and effectiveness as leaders.

Inclusive water management also benefits from recognising and valuing women's existing expertise. Women often have detailed knowledge of local water sources, seasonal variations, and water quality issues, as well as strategies for managing scarcity. Integrating this knowledge into formal water planning processes can improve the accuracy of resource assessments and the suitability of interventions.

Economic empowerment is another dimension of inclusive water management. When women are involved in planning and operating water systems, they can access opportunities for income generation, such as managing water kiosks, overseeing irrigation schemes, or leading maintenance teams. These roles can provide financial independence, enhance social status, and inspire younger generations.

Community-level governance mechanisms, such as water user associations or watershed committees, can be structured to ensure gender balance in leadership positions and decision-making processes. Legal frameworks and policies should mandate and support women's participation, backed by enforcement measures and targeted support for underrepresented groups. Partnerships between governments, NGOs, and community-based organizations can also help create enabling environments for women's leadership in water management.

The benefits of inclusive water management extend beyond gender equality. Studies show that when women are actively engaged in water governance, systems are more likely to be well-maintained, service delivery improves, and community compliance with rules increases. Women's involvement fosters a more holistic understanding of water needs, bridging household, agricultural, and environmental priorities.

Empowering women through inclusive water management is not only a matter of social justice but also a practical necessity for achieving water security and sustainable development. By dismantling barriers, building capacity, and valuing women's contributions, societies can create more resilient, equitable, and effective water management systems that serve the entire community.

Safe Sanitation Facilities in Schools and Public Institutions

Safe sanitation facilities are essential for protecting public health, ensuring dignity, and promoting inclusion in schools and public institutions. Adequate sanitation goes beyond the mere presence of toilets; it involves ensuring that facilities are hygienic, accessible, private, gender-sensitive, and safely managed. When these criteria are met, sanitation facilities can contribute to better health outcomes, higher attendance rates, and improved quality of life.

In schools, the absence of safe and appropriate sanitation facilities can significantly affect attendance and learning, particularly for girls. Without gender-segregated toilets and menstrual hygiene management (MHM) facilities, many girls miss classes during menstruation or drop out entirely. This not only limits educational attainment but also perpetuates gender inequalities. Boys, too, are affected when facilities are unhygienic or insufficient, leading to discomfort, distraction, or illness that hinders learning.

Hygienic sanitation facilities in educational settings also reduce the spread of diseases such as diarrhea, cholera, and intestinal worms, which can cause absenteeism and lower academic performance. Integrating handwashing stations with soap and water into sanitation infrastructure further strengthens these health benefits.

In public institutions—such as healthcare centers, government buildings, and transport hubs—safe sanitation is critical for service delivery and public confidence. In healthcare settings, inadequate sanitation can undermine infection prevention and control, increasing the risk of healthcare-associated infections. In workplaces and government offices, poor sanitation can affect staff productivity and discourage public use of services.

Accessibility is a key factor in designing safe sanitation facilities. Toilets should accommodate people with disabilities, older persons, and children. Features such as ramps, handrails, and sufficient space for mobility aids ensure that facilities are inclusive and usable by all. Safety is equally important; well-lit, secure facilities reduce the risk of harassment or violence, especially for women and girls.

Sustainable management of sanitation facilities in schools and public institutions requires clear roles, adequate budgets, and regular maintenance. This includes establishing cleaning schedules, ensuring a steady supply of water and hygiene materials, and setting up systems for safe waste disposal. Community and stakeholder involvement in planning and monitoring can improve accountability and ensure facilities meet local needs.

Integrating sanitation improvements into broader health, education, and infrastructure policies maximizes impact. For example, national education strategies should include targets for sanitation coverage in schools, while health policies should address facility hygiene in public buildings. Partnerships between governments, NGOs, and the private sector can mobilize resources, share expertise, and accelerate progress.

By providing safe sanitation facilities in schools and public institutions, societies can protect health, promote gender equality, enhance learning and productivity, and foster dignity for all users. These facilities are a cornerstone of inclusive, sustainable development.

Mainstreaming Equity in Water-Related SDG Implementation

Mainstreaming equity in the implementation of water-related SDGs is essential to ensure that the benefits of water security are shared fairly across all segments of society. While SDG 6 focuses explicitly on clean water and sanitation for all, the principle of equity extends across the entire SDG framework, recognising that water underpins health, livelihoods, education, gender equality, and environmental sustainability.

Equity in water management means that all people—regardless of gender, age, socio-economic status, ethnicity, disability, or geographic location—have fair access to safe, affordable, and reliable water and sanitation services. It also means that policies and investments address the needs of marginalized and vulnerable groups who are most at risk of being left behind. Without deliberate efforts to integrate equity considerations, water initiatives risk reinforcing existing inequalities rather than reducing them.

A key step in mainstreaming equity is identifying and understanding disparities in access and service quality. Disaggregated data—by income level, gender, disability status, and location—provides insight into which communities are underserved and why. Participatory needs assessments involving local stakeholders can further reveal barriers to access, from affordability challenges to discriminatory practices in governance or service provision.

Policy frameworks should explicitly priorities equitable outcomes. This includes allocating resources to areas with the greatest need, designing subsidy and tariff structures that protect low-income households, and integrating equity-focused indicators into monitoring and evaluation systems. Governance mechanisms must also be inclusive, ensuring that marginalized voices are represented in decision-making processes related to water planning, infrastructure investment, and service delivery.

In practice, mainstreaming equity requires targeted interventions. In rural areas, this might mean investing in decentralized water systems that reach remote communities. In informal urban settlements, upgrading infrastructure and securing tenure rights can improve both water access and service reliability. Special provisions may be needed for groups such as refugees, nomadic populations, or people with disabilities, whose water needs may be overlooked in standard service models.

Capacity-building and awareness-raising are equally important. Service providers, policymakers, and community leaders should be trained in equity principles, human rights-based approaches, and inclusive planning. Public campaigns can challenge discriminatory norms and promote the idea that equitable water access is a shared societal responsibility.

By embedding equity considerations into all stages of water-related SDG implementation—planning, financing, governance, and monitoring—countries can make progress toward truly universal access. This not only advances SDG 6 but also accelerates progress across multiple goals, from poverty reduction and health to gender equality and sustainable cities. Equity in water management is not just a moral imperative; it is a practical necessity for achieving sustainable and resilient development.

Chapter 5: Water for Food and Energy Security (SDGs 2 & 7)

Water is central to achieving both food and energy security, serving as a critical input for agricultural production and energy generation. In agriculture, water sustains crop growth, supports livestock, and underpins fisheries, making efficient irrigation and sustainable management essential for ensuring food availability in the face of growing demand and climate variability. Energy systems are equally dependent on water, from hydropower generation to cooling processes in thermal plants and water-intensive bioenergy production. The interdependence between water, food, and energy requires coordinated policies and investments that optimize resource use while minimizing trade-offs. Integrated approaches, such as improving irrigation efficiency, promoting renewable energy solutions that reduce water intensity, and protecting water sources from pollution, can enhance the resilience of both sectors. Strengthening this nexus is key to meeting global needs sustainably, ensuring that water supports reliable food systems and energy access without compromising long-term environmental health.

Irrigation Efficiency and Sustainable Agricultural Water Use

Agriculture accounts for the largest share of global freshwater withdrawals, making irrigation efficiency a critical factor in achieving sustainable water management. As population growth, dietary changes, and climate change intensify the demand for food and place greater pressure on water resources, improving irrigation practices becomes essential to balance agricultural productivity with long-term water security.

Irrigation efficiency refers to the ratio of water beneficially used by crops to the total water withdrawn for irrigation. Low efficiency is often the result of water losses through evaporation, runoff, and deep percolation beyond the root zone. These inefficiencies are common in traditional irrigation methods such as flood or furrow systems, which, while inexpensive and widely used, tend to apply more water than crops actually require. Excessive irrigation can also degrade soil quality, cause waterlogging, and contribute to salinization, reducing agricultural yields over time.

Improving irrigation efficiency begins with the adoption of advanced irrigation technologies. Drip irrigation delivers water directly to the root zone, minimizing evaporation and ensuring precise application. Sprinkler systems can be designed to match crop water needs more closely than surface irrigation, though they may be less efficient in hot, windy climates. Automated and sensor-based irrigation systems offer further gains by using real-time soil moisture and weather data to optimize water delivery, preventing over- or under-irrigation.

Beyond technology, on-farm management practices play a crucial role. Scheduling irrigation based on crop growth stages and water requirements helps ensure that water is applied only when and where it is needed. Crop selection also matters; choosing drought-resistant varieties or crops suited to local climate and soil conditions can reduce overall water demand. Practices such as mulching, conservation tillage, and maintaining healthy soil organic matter can improve soil moisture retention, reducing the need for supplemental irrigation.

Water reuse and recycling represent another dimension of sustainable agricultural water use. Treated wastewater, if managed safely, can supplement freshwater supplies, particularly in water-scarce regions. Similarly, capturing and storing rainwater through small-scale harvesting systems can provide a buffer during dry periods.

At a larger scale, irrigation efficiency depends on well-maintained infrastructure. Leaky canals, unlined channels, and poorly functioning gates can waste significant volumes of water before it even reaches the farm. Upgrading and maintaining conveyance systems, lining canals, and investing in efficient distribution networks can reduce losses substantially.

Institutional and policy measures are also vital for promoting sustainable water use in agriculture. Water pricing mechanisms that reflect scarcity and encourage conservation can incentivize efficiency, provided they are designed to protect smallholder farmers from undue hardship. Water allocation policies should priorities equitable distribution and ensure that environmental flows are maintained to sustain aquatic ecosystems.

Collective action through water user associations can facilitate coordinated irrigation scheduling, shared maintenance of infrastructure, and collective investment in efficiency measures. Extension services and capacity-building programs can support farmers in adopting new technologies and practices, while research and development can drive innovation in irrigation and crop management.

Climate change adaptation must be integrated into irrigation planning. Shifting precipitation patterns and rising temperatures will alter water availability and crop water requirements. Flexible irrigation systems, coupled with long-term planning that incorporates climate projections, can help ensure resilience in agricultural production.

Ultimately, improving irrigation efficiency and promoting sustainable agricultural water use is not solely a technical challenge—it is also a governance, economic, and social issue. By combining modern technology, sound management, supportive policy frameworks, and community engagement, agricultural systems can produce more food with less water, safeguarding both food security and freshwater resources for future generations.

Nexus Thinking: Water–Energy–Food Linkages

Nexus thinking recognises that water, energy, and food systems are deeply interconnected, and that actions in one domain inevitably affect the others. This integrated perspective is essential for sustainable resource management, particularly as global demand for all three increases due to population growth, economic development, and climate change. By understanding and managing these linkages, policymakers and practitioners can identify synergies, minimize trade-offs, and ensure that resource use supports long-term sustainability.

Water is fundamental to both energy and food production. In agriculture, it is used for irrigation, livestock, and food processing. In the energy sector, water is required for cooling in thermal power plants, hydropower generation, biofuel cultivation, and fossil fuel extraction. Conversely, energy is essential for water supply and treatment—powering pumps for irrigation, desalination plants, and wastewater treatment facilities. Food production also consumes energy at multiple stages, from fertilizer manufacturing and mechanized farming to transportation and storage.

These interdependencies mean that inefficiencies or shortages in one system can cascade into others. For example, over-extraction of water for irrigation can reduce availability for hydropower generation, while energy shortages can disrupt water pumping for agriculture, threatening food security. Similarly, producing more bioenergy crops to meet renewable energy targets may compete with food crops for land and water, potentially raising food prices and increasing water stress.

Climate change intensifies these challenges. Shifts in precipitation patterns affect water availability for both crops and energy production, while extreme weather events can disrupt supply chains across all three sectors. Rising temperatures increase irrigation needs, energy demand for cooling, and stress on ecosystems, making integrated planning even more critical.

Nexus thinking promotes coordinated approaches that optimize resource use across sectors. For instance, improving irrigation efficiency can reduce both water and energy consumption, as less water needs to be pumped and treated. Deploying renewable energy for water supply—such as solar-powered pumps—can lower greenhouse gas emissions and improve reliability in off-grid rural areas. Similarly, reusing treated wastewater for agriculture or cooling can reduce freshwater withdrawals, supporting both food and energy systems.

Policy and governance frameworks are key to operationalizing the nexus approach. Traditional sectoral planning often overlooks cross-sectoral impacts, leading to conflicting policies or unintended consequences. Integrated planning, supported by cross-ministerial coordination and shared data systems, can align objectives across water, energy, and food sectors. Economic instruments such as pricing reforms, incentives for efficiency, and investment in multipurpose infrastructure can further promote nexus-friendly solutions.

Stakeholder engagement is another cornerstone of the nexus approach. Farmers, utilities, industries, and communities all have a stake in how resources are managed. Collaborative platforms can foster dialogue, share knowledge, and build consensus on trade-offs and co-benefits.

By embracing nexus thinking, societies can transition from fragmented resource management to a more holistic, resilient model. This approach not only enhances efficiency and reduces environmental impacts but also strengthens food security, energy reliability, and water sustainability—ensuring that these critical systems can support human well-being and economic development in a resource-constrained world.

Renewable Energy and Water Interdependencies

The transition to renewable energy is a cornerstone of global efforts to mitigate climate change, but it also presents important interdependencies with water resources. While renewable energy sources generally have a lower water footprint than fossil fuel–based power generation, they are not entirely water-independent. Understanding and managing these interconnections is essential to ensure that the expansion of renewable energy supports both energy security and sustainable water management.

Hydropower is the most prominent example of water-dependent renewable energy. It relies directly on the availability and flow of freshwater to generate electricity. While hydropower offers a low-carbon energy source, it can have significant implications for water allocation, ecosystem health, and downstream users. Seasonal variability, drought, and climate change–driven shifts in precipitation patterns can affect generation capacity, creating potential conflicts between energy production, agriculture, and municipal water supply. Conversely, strategic reservoir management can support multiple objectives, including flood control, irrigation, and drought mitigation.

Bioenergy, including biofuels from crops such as maize, sugarcane, and oilseeds, also requires substantial water inputs, both for cultivation and processing. Large-scale bioenergy production can compete with food crops for water and land, potentially exacerbating water scarcity in regions already under stress. Efficient irrigation, the use of drought-tolerant crops, and careful siting of bioenergy production can help reduce these impacts, but trade-offs remain.

Geothermal energy has moderate water requirements, primarily for cooling and reinjection processes. While it can operate with relatively low freshwater consumption compared to fossil fuels, managing water quality is critical to prevent contamination from dissolved minerals and other substances extracted during operation.

Solar and wind power are generally considered low-water-use technologies, particularly photovoltaic (PV) solar panels and wind turbines, which require minimal water for operation. However, some solar technologies—such as concentrated solar power (CSP)—require water for cooling and steam generation, which can be significant in certain configurations. In water-scarce areas, dry cooling or hybrid systems can help reduce demand, albeit often at higher cost or lower efficiency.

The water–energy interdependency also flows in the opposite direction: renewable energy can improve water security. Solar-powered pumps, wind-powered desalination systems, and renewable-powered wastewater treatment plants can provide reliable water services in off-grid or remote areas, reducing reliance on fossil fuels and lowering operational costs. In agriculture, renewable energy can power efficient irrigation systems, improving productivity while minimizing environmental impact.

Planning for renewable energy deployment must therefore account for local water availability, competing demands, and potential climate impacts. Integrated resource planning that considers both water and energy needs can help identify synergies and avoid conflicts. For example, pairing renewable energy projects with water reuse systems can create closed-loop solutions that conserve both resources.

As countries scale up renewable energy, managing the water dimension will be essential to ensure sustainable, resilient systems. This means not only minimizing the water footprint of renewable technologies but also leveraging them to enhance water access, quality, and reliability. By aligning renewable energy expansion with sound water management, societies can advance climate, energy, and water security goals in tandem.

Addressing Competing Demands and Trade-Offs

Water is a finite resource subject to competing demands from multiple sectors, including agriculture, energy, industry, households, and the environment. Balancing these demands is a central challenge for achieving water security and meeting broader sustainable development objectives. Trade-offs are inevitable, particularly in regions facing water scarcity, but they can be managed through integrated planning, equitable allocation, and efficient use.

Agriculture is typically the largest water user, especially in developing countries, where irrigation supports food production and rural livelihoods. However, diverting large volumes of water to farming can reduce availability for domestic consumption, industrial activities, and environmental flows. Energy production, whether from hydropower, thermal plants, or bioenergy crops, also competes for water, creating tensions between water and energy security. Industrial sectors, including manufacturing, mining, and processing, require reliable water supplies for production processes, while urban populations need safe water for drinking, sanitation, and hygiene.

Environmental needs often receive less priority in allocation decisions, yet maintaining healthy ecosystems is essential for long-term water sustainability. Wetlands, rivers, and aquifers provide critical services such as water filtration, flood regulation, and biodiversity support. Over-extraction for human uses can degrade these systems, leading to irreversible ecological damage and reduced resilience to climate change.

Trade-offs can also arise within sectors. For example, decisions about allocating water among different crops may priorities high-value exports over staple foods, affecting food security. Similarly, energy planners may favor water-intensive generation technologies without considering implications for other sectors during drought periods.

Addressing these competing demands requires a combination of strategies. Integrated Water Resources Management (IWRM) provides a framework for coordinating water allocation across sectors and scales, considering social, economic, and environmental objectives. Water pricing and allocation policies can incentivize efficiency and signal the true value of water, while ensuring that basic needs and vulnerable groups are protected through subsidies or targeted support.

Technological innovations can reduce competition by improving water efficiency and enabling reuse. For instance, drip irrigation minimizes agricultural water use, closed-loop cooling systems reduce industrial withdrawals, and wastewater recycling can supply non-potable needs, freeing up freshwater for other uses.

Stakeholder engagement is crucial to building consensus around allocation decisions and managing trade-offs transparently. Inclusive decision-making processes allow diverse interests to be represented, helping to identify mutually beneficial solutions and reduce the risk of conflict. Scenario planning and modelling can further support decision-makers by illustrating the impacts of different allocation choices under varying climate, economic, and demographic conditions.

By recognising interdependencies, prioritizing equity, and fostering collaboration, it is possible to manage competing demands in ways that balance immediate needs with long-term sustainability. Such approaches ensure that water allocation supports economic development, social well-being, and environmental integrity, even in the face of growing pressures.

Enhancing Productivity Through Integrated Resource Management

Integrated Resource Management (IRM) is a holistic approach that coordinates the use and management of water, land, energy, and other natural resources to maximize productivity while ensuring sustainability. By recognising the interconnections between sectors, IRM seeks to optimize resource use, minimize waste, and deliver economic, social, and environmental benefits simultaneously.

In agriculture, integrating water, soil, and nutrient management can significantly boost productivity. Efficient irrigation techniques—such as drip or sprinkler systems—combined with soil moisture monitoring ensure that crops receive the right amount of water at the right time. This reduces losses from over-irrigation and enhances yields. Complementary practices like crop rotation, conservation tillage, and the use of organic matter improve soil structure and water retention, further reducing water demand. Linking these measures with renewable energy sources for pumping or processing strengthens resource efficiency and resilience.

In energy and industry, integrated approaches focus on reducing water and energy footprints simultaneously. For example, industries can adopt closed-loop cooling systems, water recycling, and energy-efficient production processes. These measures not only conserve resources but also lower operational costs. Co-locating facilities—such as pairing power plants with wastewater treatment plants—can create synergies where waste heat or treated water from one process becomes an input for another.

Urban settings also benefit from IRM through water-sensitive urban design, which integrates stormwater management, green infrastructure, and efficient supply systems. Measures such as rainwater harvesting, wastewater reuse, and permeable surfaces reduce pressure on centralized infrastructure while supporting urban greening and climate resilience. These solutions enhance the livability of cities and reduce resource waste.

At the governance level, IRM requires cross-sectoral coordination among water, agriculture, energy, environment, and urban planning authorities. Policies should incentivize integrated solutions—such as subsidies for multi-purpose infrastructure, regulatory frameworks that enable resource reuse, and investment in data systems that track flows across sectors. Decision-making should be based on shared resource assessments that account for cumulative impacts and potential trade-offs.

Capacity-building is essential to enable farmers, industries, and municipalities to adopt integrated practices. Training, technology transfer, and access to finance can accelerate uptake. Public–private partnerships can also play a role in developing and scaling integrated solutions, particularly in resource-intensive sectors.

By managing resources in an integrated manner, productivity gains are achieved not just through higher outputs but also through reduced inputs and environmental impacts. This creates more resilient systems that can adapt to changing climate conditions, fluctuating market demands, and growing population pressures. Ultimately, IRM fosters sustainable growth by ensuring that resource use today does not compromise the ability of future generations to meet their needs.

Chapter 6: Sustainable Water Use and Economic Growth (SDG 8)

Sustainable water use is essential for fostering long-term economic growth under SDG 8, which calls for inclusive and sustainable economic development, full and productive employment, and decent work for all. Water underpins key economic sectors, including agriculture, industry, energy, and tourism, making its availability and quality a determinant of productivity and competitiveness. Overexploitation, pollution, and inefficient allocation can create bottlenecks, hinder investment, and increase operational risks for businesses. Sustainable water management ensures that economic expansion is supported by reliable supply, resilient infrastructure, and ecosystem protection. Investments in water efficiency, wastewater reuse, and circular economy approaches can generate green jobs, stimulate innovation, and reduce costs for enterprises. By integrating water considerations into economic planning, governments and businesses can safeguard resources, enhance resilience to climate and market shocks, and promote growth that benefits both people and the environment, ensuring prosperity without degrading the natural capital on which economies depend.

Water as a Driver of Economic Activity and Productivity

Water is a fundamental enabler of economic growth and productivity across all sectors of society. Its role extends far beyond meeting basic human needs—it is integral to agriculture, industry, energy generation, transportation, and a wide range of services. When water resources are reliable, well-managed, and equitably distributed, they provide a stable foundation for economic development. Conversely, water scarcity, poor quality, or unreliable supply can constrain productivity, increase costs, and limit opportunities for growth.

In agriculture, which remains the largest global water user, reliable water access is essential for crop production, livestock rearing, and aquaculture. Irrigation enables farmers to overcome rainfall variability, extend growing seasons, and cultivate higher-value crops. This not only increases yields but also stabilizes incomes and supports rural employment. Agricultural productivity, in turn, feeds into food security, export earnings, and the growth of agro-processing industries. Efficient water use in agriculture can also free up resources for other sectors, enhancing overall economic resilience.

Industry depends heavily on water for production processes, cooling, cleaning, and product formulation. Sectors such as textiles, chemicals, food and beverages, pharmaceuticals, and electronics require consistent water quality and quantity to maintain output and meet regulatory standards. Access to reliable water supplies supports industrial competitiveness, encourages investment, and allows for the expansion of manufacturing capacity. Conversely, disruptions in water supply can halt production lines, damage equipment, and result in significant financial losses.

In the energy sector, water plays a critical role in both renewable and non-renewable generation. Hydropower directly converts water flow into electricity, while thermal power plants—whether coal, gas, nuclear, or concentrated solar—require water for cooling. Bioenergy production relies on water for crop cultivation, and even wind and solar photovoltaic supply chains have water footprints in manufacturing stages. Energy, in turn, powers water supply and treatment systems, creating a mutually dependent relationship that must be managed to optimize efficiency and reliability.

Water is also central to the service economy. Tourism, particularly in coastal, lake, or riverine areas, relies on clean, attractive water bodies. Hospitality services require secure water supplies for guests, food preparation, and facility maintenance. Similarly, healthcare systems depend on safe water for patient care, hygiene, and sanitation. In transport, navigable rivers and canals facilitate the movement of goods and people, linking economic hubs and reducing freight costs.

Beyond sector-specific contributions, water security fosters economic productivity by creating a stable environment for investment. Businesses are more likely to expand operations in areas where water risks are well managed. Adequate water infrastructure—such as storage facilities, treatment plants, and distribution networks—reduces the costs associated with supply interruptions and enhances resilience to droughts and floods.

The economic benefits of water are not limited to direct use. Healthy aquatic ecosystems provide services such as flood regulation, groundwater recharge, nutrient cycling, and fisheries, all of which support livelihoods and contribute to economic stability. Degradation of these systems through over-extraction or pollution can undermine long-term productivity and increase the costs of restoration.

Realizing water's potential as a driver of economic activity requires integrated management that aligns supply with sustainable demand. Investment in water-efficient technologies, infrastructure maintenance, and pollution control enhances reliability and reduces waste. Pricing mechanisms that reflect the value of water can encourage conservation and reallocation to higher-value uses, while protecting affordability for basic needs.

Moreover, policies must address equity and inclusion, ensuring that economic benefits from water use are widely shared. This involves extending services to underserved communities, supporting small-scale producers, and engaging local stakeholders in decision-making.

When managed sustainably, water is not just a supporting input but a strategic asset that drives productivity, fosters innovation, and underpins long-term economic growth. As pressures on water resources increase, recognising and maximizing its economic value will be critical for building resilient, competitive, and inclusive economies.

Industrial Water Use and Sustainable Business Practices

Industry is a major user of water, relying on it for manufacturing processes, cooling, cleaning, product formulation, and sanitation. Sectors such as textiles, chemicals, pulp and paper, food and beverage, pharmaceuticals, and electronics are particularly water-intensive, requiring both high volumes and specific water quality standards. Industrial water use not only supports economic output and employment but also has significant implications for local water resources, ecosystems, and communities.

In many regions, industrial growth has increased competition for water with agriculture, households, and the environment. Poorly managed industrial withdrawals can strain local supplies, while untreated or inadequately treated wastewater can degrade water quality, harming public health and biodiversity. As water scarcity becomes more pressing due to population growth, urbanization, and climate change, industries face growing operational and reputational risks linked to water use.

Sustainable business practices aim to reduce these risks while improving efficiency, resilience, and social license to operate. One key strategy is improving water-use efficiency through process optimization and technology upgrades. Closed-loop systems, where water is recycled within the production process, can drastically reduce withdrawals. Switching to dry or low-water processes—for example, in cooling or cleaning—also helps lower consumption.

Wastewater treatment and reuse are central to sustainable industrial water management. On-site treatment facilities allow companies to meet regulatory discharge standards and recover water for non-potable uses, such as cooling or irrigation. Advanced treatment technologies, including membrane filtration and reverse osmosis, can enable high-quality water recycling, reducing reliance on freshwater sources.

Industries can also adopt circular economy principles by recovering valuable by-products from wastewater, such as heat, nutrients, or chemicals. This not only improves resource efficiency but can generate additional revenue streams. Implementing water stewardship programs—where companies work collaboratively with other water users and stakeholders—helps address shared challenges at the watershed level, supporting long-term water security for all.

Transparent monitoring and reporting are important for accountability and performance improvement. Measuring water withdrawals, consumption, and discharge quality enables companies to set targets, track progress, and identify opportunities for further reduction. Many businesses now align with global disclosure frameworks, such as the CDP Water Security questionnaire, to communicate their water performance to investors and the public.

Engaging suppliers is another critical aspect, particularly for companies whose water footprint extends far beyond direct operations. Encouraging or requiring sustainable water practices in supply chains can reduce overall risk and strengthen resilience. This is especially relevant in sectors like apparel and food production, where agricultural inputs account for a large share of water use.

Regulatory compliance remains a baseline requirement, but leading companies go further by setting voluntary commitments, adopting international standards such as the Alliance for Water Stewardship (AWS) Standard, and integrating water risk assessments into business strategy.

By reducing consumption, improving wastewater management, and engaging in collaborative stewardship, industries can align profitability with environmental and social responsibility. Sustainable water practices not only protect the resource base on which businesses depend but also enhance operational resilience, reduce costs, and strengthen brand reputation in an increasingly water-conscious world.

Job Creation Through Water Infrastructure and Services

Investment in water infrastructure and services is a powerful driver of job creation, contributing to both immediate employment and long-term economic development. The water sector encompasses a wide range of activities, including the construction, operation, and maintenance of water supply systems, wastewater treatment facilities, irrigation networks, stormwater management systems, and nature-based solutions. These activities generate jobs directly within the sector and indirectly through the economic opportunities they enable in other industries.

Direct job creation occurs during the planning, design, and construction phases of water infrastructure projects. Engineers, construction workers, equipment operators, and project managers are employed to build dams, treatment plants, pipelines, reservoirs, and distribution systems. These projects also stimulate demand for goods and services from related sectors such as manufacturing (pipes, pumps, filtration systems), transport, and logistics. The scale of employment can be significant during major infrastructure rollouts or rehabilitation programs.

Once infrastructure is operational, ongoing jobs are created in operations and maintenance. Water treatment plant operators, maintenance technicians, meter readers, and customer service personnel are essential to keeping systems functioning effectively. The adoption of advanced technologies, such as smart meters and automated monitoring, is creating new roles in data management, systems analysis, and technical support.

Water services also contribute indirectly to job creation by enabling economic activities in other sectors. Reliable water supply supports agricultural production, food processing, manufacturing, energy generation, and tourism, all of which employ large numbers of people. For example, irrigated agriculture not only sustains farm jobs but also supports employment in input supply chains, transport, and marketing. Similarly, improved water quality and sanitation boost public health, reducing absenteeism and increasing workforce productivity.

Nature-based water infrastructure—such as wetland restoration, watershed management, and green urban drainage systems—generates jobs in environmental management, forestry, landscaping, and conservation. These projects often rely on local labor and can provide employment in rural or disadvantaged communities, aligning environmental restoration with socio-economic benefits.

Investments in water infrastructure can also promote skills development and capacity-building. Training programs in plumbing, leak detection, water quality testing, and system maintenance equip workers with marketable skills that are transferable to other sectors. Public–private partnerships, donor-funded initiatives, and municipal programs often incorporate vocational training to ensure a skilled workforce for the long term.

The job creation potential of water projects can be maximized by designing them with inclusive employment strategies. This includes promoting gender equality in recruitment, providing opportunities for youth and marginalized groups, and ensuring fair wages and safe working conditions. Community-based approaches to water management can further enhance local employment while fostering ownership and sustainability.

By coupling infrastructure investment with policies that priorities inclusive and sustainable employment, governments and development partners can multiply the socio-economic benefits of water sector spending. In doing so, they not only address critical water security challenges but also stimulate economic growth, enhance livelihoods, and contribute to achieving broader development goals.

Valuing Water in Economic Policy and Investment Decisions

Valuing water in economic policy and investment decisions is essential for ensuring that this finite resource is allocated, used, and protected in ways that support long-term sustainability, equity, and economic growth. Water underpins virtually every sector of the economy, yet it is often undervalued in decision-making, leading to inefficiencies, overuse, and environmental degradation. By recognising its full economic, social, and environmental value, policymakers and investors can make more informed choices that balance competing needs.

Economic valuation of water involves assessing its multiple benefits—direct and indirect, tangible and intangible. Direct benefits include its role in agriculture, industry, energy generation, and domestic supply. Indirect benefits include ecosystem services such as water filtration, flood regulation, and habitat provision, which support biodiversity and climate resilience. Incorporating these values into policy ensures that water is not treated as an unlimited, free resource but as a strategic asset.

One of the most effective tools for valuing water is pricing that reflects its true cost of delivery and the opportunity cost of its use. While pricing must remain affordable for basic human needs, setting tariffs that account for infrastructure maintenance, treatment, and environmental protection can encourage efficient use and generate revenue for reinvestment. Tiered pricing structures, lifeline tariffs, and targeted subsidies can balance equity and cost recovery.

In investment decisions, valuing water means integrating water risk assessments into project planning and financing. Infrastructure projects, industrial developments, and agricultural expansions should evaluate how water availability, quality, and climate variability might affect operations and long-term viability. Investors are increasingly recognising water risk as a material financial issue, influencing lending terms, insurance premiums, and corporate valuations.

Valuation also plays a role in prioritizing investments. Projects that deliver multiple water-related benefits—such as wastewater reuse systems that also generate energy, or watershed restoration that improves supply reliability and biodiversity—offer higher overall returns when all benefits are considered. Cost–benefit analyses that include environmental and social impacts can shift investment toward more sustainable options.

International frameworks, such as the United Nations' *Valuing Water Principles*, encourage holistic approaches that consider equity, ecosystem integrity, and resilience alongside economic efficiency. Applying these principles can help align water-related decisions with the Sustainable Development Goals and climate commitments.

Ultimately, valuing water in policy and investment decisions requires robust data, transparent governance, and stakeholder participation. By making the true value of water visible in economic terms while safeguarding its social and environmental dimensions, decision-makers can ensure that water supports sustainable growth, equitable access, and resilience for generations to come.

Fostering Green Jobs and Circular Water Economies

The transition to sustainable water management presents a significant opportunity to foster green jobs and advance circular water economies. Green jobs in the water sector contribute to environmental protection, resource efficiency, and resilience, while circular water economies aim to close resource loops by reusing, recycling, and recovering water and related by-products. Together, these approaches support sustainable development, create employment, and strengthen water security.

Green jobs in water span a wide range of activities. They include roles in the design, construction, and maintenance of water-efficient infrastructure; the operation of advanced treatment plants; and the implementation of technologies for wastewater reuse and stormwater harvesting. Restoration projects—such as wetland rehabilitation, watershed management, and green urban drainage—also provide employment, often drawing on local labor and delivering both environmental and socio-economic benefits.

Circular water economies focus on maximizing the value of water by keeping it in use for as long as possible. This includes recovering water from wastewater for non-potable uses such as irrigation, industrial processes, or cooling; capturing stormwater for reuse; and recycling process water within industrial systems. The approach also extends to recovering valuable resources from water streams, such as nutrients for fertilizer, biogas from sludge, or heat energy from wastewater. Each of these activities creates specialized jobs in engineering, operations, monitoring, and environmental management.

Innovation is a key driver in expanding both green jobs and circular water practices. Emerging fields such as digital water management, smart metering, and decentralized treatment systems require skilled professionals in data analysis, systems integration, and technology deployment. Research and development roles contribute to advancing more efficient, cost-effective, and scalable solutions, while training and education programs equip workers with the skills needed for a rapidly evolving sector.

Policy and investment frameworks play a pivotal role in fostering growth in this area. Governments can incentivize green job creation and circular water initiatives through supportive regulations, funding for sustainable infrastructure, and inclusion of circular economy principles in water policy. Public–private partnerships can accelerate innovation and expand market opportunities, while vocational training programs ensure that local communities benefit directly from employment opportunities.

The benefits of fostering green jobs and circular water economies extend beyond employment and environmental gains. By reducing water withdrawals, minimizing waste, and recovering valuable resources, these approaches enhance resilience to water scarcity, lower costs for businesses and municipalities, and reduce greenhouse gas emissions.

Integrating green job creation with circular water strategies offers a pathway to sustainable, inclusive growth. By aligning economic development with environmental stewardship, societies can protect vital water resources while generating new opportunities for work and innovation in a changing global economy.

Chapter 7: Water and Sustainable Cities (SDG 11)

Water is central to the vision of sustainable cities under SDG 11, which seeks to make urban areas inclusive, safe, resilient, and sustainable. As cities grow, they face mounting challenges in securing adequate water supplies, managing wastewater, and protecting against flooding and drought. Urban water security depends on resilient infrastructure, effective governance, and integrated planning that balances demand with sustainable supply. Pollution control, stormwater management, and investments in both grey and green infrastructure are essential for maintaining healthy urban water systems. Equitable access to safe water and sanitation services ensures that vulnerable communities are not left behind, while efficient resource use reduces pressure on surrounding ecosystems. Water-sensitive urban design can enhance climate resilience, improve livability, and create co-benefits such as green spaces and biodiversity. By embedding sustainable water management into urban development strategies, cities can thrive while safeguarding the resources needed for future generations.

Urban Water Security Challenges: Demand, Pollution, Infrastructure Gaps

Urban water security is a growing concern worldwide, driven by rapid population growth, economic expansion, and the increasing impacts of climate change. Cities concentrate people, industries, and services, placing high demands on water resources while generating significant pollution loads. At the same time, many urban areas face ageing or inadequate infrastructure, creating systemic vulnerabilities that threaten reliable, safe, and equitable water access.

Urbanization increases water demand for households, commerce, industry, and public services. Expanding populations require more drinking water, sanitation, and hygiene facilities, while industrial and service sectors often compete for the same resources. Rising living standards can further amplify demand through increased water use for appliances, landscaping, and leisure activities. In many cities, water demand is outpacing the capacity of supply systems, particularly in regions with limited freshwater resources. Climate change compounds the problem, as rising temperatures and altered precipitation patterns can increase water needs for cooling, irrigation of urban green spaces, and other adaptive measures.

Urban areas are major sources of water pollution, with untreated or inadequately treated wastewater being a primary contributor. Domestic sewage, industrial effluents, and stormwater runoff carry pathogens, nutrients, heavy metals, and other contaminants into rivers, lakes, and coastal waters. Informal settlements without adequate sanitation systems often discharge waste directly into the environment, exacerbating public health risks. Industrial discharges can degrade water quality, affecting both human and ecosystem health, and in some cases rendering water sources unfit for supply without costly treatment. Stormwater runoff from impervious surfaces, such as roads and rooftops, can carry pollutants and cause flash flooding, further straining urban drainage systems.

Many cities face significant challenges related to water infrastructure. In rapidly growing urban areas, infrastructure expansion has often failed to keep pace with demand, leaving underserved communities reliant on informal or unsafe water sources. In older cities, ageing infrastructure leads to high rates of water loss through leaks, frequent service interruptions, and contamination risks from corroded pipes. Inadequate wastewater treatment capacity is another critical gap, resulting in environmental degradation and lost opportunities for water reuse.

Financing infrastructure improvements remains a persistent challenge. Large-scale investments are required to expand coverage, upgrade ageing systems, and incorporate climate-resilient designs, but budget constraints, governance weaknesses, and competing priorities can delay progress. Furthermore, infrastructure projects that focus solely on supply expansion without addressing demand management or efficiency can exacerbate long-term sustainability issues.

Urban water insecurity disproportionately affects low-income and marginalized communities. Informal settlements often lack piped water connections and adequate sanitation, forcing residents to rely on costly water vendors or unsafe sources. Service inequalities can deepen social divides, perpetuating cycles of poverty and limiting economic opportunities. Ensuring equitable access requires targeted policies, subsidies, and participatory planning that address the needs of underserved groups.

Improving urban water security requires integrated strategies that address demand, pollution, and infrastructure simultaneously. Demand management measures, such as water-efficient appliances, leak reduction, pricing reforms, and public awareness campaigns, can help curb consumption. Pollution control requires expanding wastewater treatment coverage, enforcing industrial discharge regulations, and implementing green infrastructure to manage stormwater sustainably.

Investments in infrastructure should priorities resilience, ensuring systems can withstand climate-related shocks such as floods, droughts, and extreme heat. This may involve diversifying supply sources through rainwater harvesting, desalination, or reclaimed wastewater, as well as modernizing distribution networks to reduce losses.

Governance and institutional capacity are equally critical. Coordinated planning between water utilities, urban planners, environmental agencies, and community stakeholders can foster more effective and inclusive solutions. Strengthening financing mechanisms—through public–private partnerships, municipal bonds, and international funding—can help bridge investment gaps.

By tackling demand pressures, reducing pollution, and closing infrastructure gaps, cities can move toward a future where water is managed efficiently, equitably, and sustainably. Urban water security is not only a prerequisite for public health and environmental quality but also a foundation for economic resilience and social stability.

Resilient Urban Design and Water-Sensitive Planning

Resilient urban design and water-sensitive planning are essential approaches for addressing the growing pressures of climate change, urbanization, and water scarcity in cities. By integrating water management into the fabric of urban design, these approaches aim to create cities that can withstand shocks such as floods, droughts, and heatwaves, while enhancing livability, environmental health, and social equity.

Resilient urban design focuses on creating built environments that can absorb, adapt to, and recover from disruptions. In the context of water, this means designing infrastructure, landscapes, and public spaces that manage water sustainably, minimize flood risk, and maintain supply security during periods of scarcity. Resilience requires both physical measures—such as robust drainage systems and climate-ready water supply networks—and social measures, including community engagement, governance, and preparedness.

Water-sensitive planning is closely aligned, placing water management at the heart of urban development. It recognizes the water cycle as a key organizing principle for land use and infrastructure decisions, integrating water supply, wastewater, stormwater, and environmental flows into a single planning framework. This approach moves beyond traditional engineering solutions to embrace natural processes, green infrastructure, and multi-functional urban spaces.

Green infrastructure is a central feature of water-sensitive planning. Parks, wetlands, bioswales, rain gardens, and green roofs help capture, store, and filter rainwater, reducing stormwater runoff and mitigating flood risk. These systems also enhance biodiversity, improve air quality, and provide recreational spaces. By mimicking natural hydrology, they complement traditional drainage systems, making urban water management more adaptable and cost-effective.

Decentralized water solutions are another important element. Localized rainwater harvesting, greywater recycling, and small-scale treatment systems can reduce dependence on centralized infrastructure, increase supply resilience, and lower the environmental footprint of water services. These solutions are particularly valuable in informal settlements and rapidly expanding peri-urban areas, where extending traditional networks can be costly and time-consuming.

Resilient urban design also involves considering climate change projections in all stages of planning and construction. This includes building in areas less prone to flooding, designing permeable surfaces to improve infiltration, and incorporating water-efficient landscaping to reduce irrigation needs. Strategic zoning can protect water-sensitive areas, such as wetlands and recharge zones, from development pressures.

Community engagement is vital to the success of water-sensitive planning. Residents, businesses, and civic organizations must be involved in shaping solutions, as their cooperation is crucial for maintaining systems and changing behaviors. Education campaigns can promote water conservation, flood preparedness, and the value of green spaces.

Policy and governance frameworks must support integration across sectors and scales. This requires coordination between water utilities, urban planners, environmental agencies, and developers, along with supportive regulations and incentives for sustainable design practices.

By embedding resilience and water sensitivity into urban planning, cities can not only manage risks more effectively but also create vibrant, healthy, and inclusive environments. These approaches offer long-term economic, social, and environmental benefits, making them essential strategies for sustainable urban futures.

Wastewater Reuse, Stormwater Management, and Flood Resilience

Integrating wastewater reuse, stormwater management, and flood resilience into urban planning is essential for building cities that are resource-efficient, climate-adapted, and water-secure. These three elements are interlinked: effective wastewater treatment enables safe reuse, stormwater management reduces pollution and flood risks, and flood resilience safeguards infrastructure, communities, and economies from extreme weather events.

Wastewater reuse transforms a waste product into a valuable resource. When treated to appropriate standards, reclaimed water can be used for non-potable purposes such as agricultural irrigation, industrial cooling, landscape watering, and replenishing groundwater aquifers. In some cases, advanced treatment allows for potable reuse, directly supplementing drinking water supplies. This approach reduces demand on freshwater sources, lowers the energy footprint of long-distance water transfers, and decreases pollutant loads discharged into natural waterways.

Successful wastewater reuse depends on reliable treatment infrastructure, rigorous water quality monitoring, and clear regulatory frameworks that define allowable uses and safety standards. Public acceptance is also crucial, requiring transparent communication about treatment processes, health safeguards, and benefits. Investment in decentralized or modular treatment systems can bring reuse opportunities to neighborhoods or industrial parks, particularly in rapidly urbanizing areas.

Urbanization increases impervious surfaces, which prevent rainfall from naturally infiltrating into the ground. As a result, stormwater runs off quickly, often carrying pollutants such as oil, heavy metals, nutrients, and litter into waterways. Poorly managed stormwater can overwhelm drainage systems, cause localized flooding, and degrade water quality.

Modern stormwater management incorporates green infrastructure—such as bioswales, rain gardens, permeable pavements, and green roofs—that slows, filters, and stores runoff. These systems mimic natural hydrology, allowing infiltration and evapotranspiration to reduce runoff volumes and improve water quality. Detention and retention basins can store stormwater for controlled release, while also creating recreational and ecological spaces.

Integrating stormwater capture into reuse schemes further enhances efficiency. Collected stormwater can be treated and used for irrigation, industrial processes, or groundwater recharge, reducing dependence on potable supplies.

Flood resilience aims to reduce the impacts of extreme rainfall and riverine or coastal flooding, which are becoming more frequent and severe due to climate change. Resilient cities employ both structural and non-structural measures. Structural measures include levees, sea walls, retention basins, and upgraded drainage systems, while non-structural measures encompass land-use planning, early warning systems, and community preparedness.

Nature-based solutions can play a dual role in flood resilience and water management. Restored wetlands, riparian buffers, and urban green corridors absorb excess water, slow runoff, and provide habitat. These measures often cost less and deliver more co-benefits than hard infrastructure alone.

Linking wastewater reuse, stormwater management, and flood resilience creates synergies that optimize resource use and strengthen urban water security. For example, stormwater captured in flood-prone areas can be treated for reuse, reducing both flood risk and water demand. Planning these systems together encourages multi-purpose infrastructure, maximizes return on investment, and enhances climate adaptation.

Cities that adopt an integrated approach to these three elements can reduce environmental impacts, bolster water supplies, and improve their capacity to withstand and recover from extreme events—contributing to a safer, more sustainable urban future.

Urban-Rural Water Flows and Metropolitan Water Footprints

Urban-rural water flows represent the interconnected nature of water systems, where cities depend on surrounding and often distant rural areas for their water supply, while rural economies benefit from urban markets, infrastructure, and investment. This relationship also includes virtual water—the water embedded in the production of food, goods, and energy consumed in cities. As metropolitan populations grow and economies expand, demand for water-intensive goods and services increases, influencing the overall water footprint of urban areas.

Most metropolitan regions rely on surface water and groundwater sources located outside their administrative boundaries, with large-scale conveyance systems transporting water from rural catchments, reservoirs, or rivers, sometimes over hundreds of kilometers. These flows can put pressure on rural water resources, especially when upstream agricultural, ecological, or community needs compete with urban demand. In water-scarce regions, urban withdrawals can contribute to declining aquifers, reduced river flows, and ecosystem degradation.

While rural areas can benefit economically from supplying water—through infrastructure investments, employment in water management, and access to urban markets—there are also potential negative impacts. Water diversion for urban consumption can limit agricultural production, affect local livelihoods, and disrupt traditional water governance systems. Fair water allocation, compensation mechanisms, and investment in rural water infrastructure are therefore essential to maintaining balanced relationships between urban and rural stakeholders.

A metropolitan water footprint measures the total volume of freshwater consumed, both directly within the city and indirectly through goods and services produced elsewhere. This includes domestic water use, industrial processes, and embedded water in food, textiles, energy, and manufactured goods. A significant portion of this footprint is tied to agricultural production in rural regions, often far from the city itself. Understanding and managing metropolitan water footprints requires comprehensive accounting and transparency across supply chains. By identifying the largest contributors to water use, cities can collaborate with suppliers, farmers, and industries to adopt more efficient practices, reduce waste, and shift towards less water-intensive consumption patterns.

Sustainable management of urban-rural water flows depends on collaborative governance that accounts for hydrological, economic, and social interdependencies. Integrated water resources management approaches can help balance competing needs, improve efficiency, and protect ecosystem health. Investments in water recycling, demand management, and alternative sources—such as rainwater harvesting and desalination—can reduce pressure on rural water supplies. Recognising the scale and impact of their water footprints enables metropolitan areas to take responsibility for their broader resource use, fostering partnerships that ensure resilient and equitable water systems across both urban and rural landscapes.

Governance for Inclusive, Sustainable Urban Water Systems

Governance plays a central role in shaping how urban water systems are planned, financed, and managed to meet the needs of diverse populations while safeguarding long-term sustainability. Effective governance ensures that all residents—regardless of income, location, or social status—have reliable access to safe water and sanitation. It also addresses the environmental pressures of urbanization, population growth, and climate change, aligning service delivery with ecological integrity and resource efficiency.

Inclusive governance requires decision-making processes that actively involve multiple stakeholders, including local communities, civil society, utilities, the private sector, and government agencies. Public participation enhances transparency, builds trust, and ensures that water policies reflect the realities of different user groups. Special attention must be given to marginalized communities, informal settlements, and peri-urban areas, where service gaps are often most pronounced. Mechanisms such as participatory planning, social audits, and grievance redress systems can help ensure that service provision is equitable and responsive.

Sustainability within urban water systems depends on integrated planning that connects water supply, sanitation, drainage, and environmental management. This requires coordination across sectors such as housing, energy, transport, and land use. Regulatory frameworks must support efficient water use, protect water sources from pollution, and incentivize investment in resilient infrastructure. Financial sustainability is also critical, with tariffs, subsidies, and funding mechanisms designed to recover costs while protecting affordability for low-income households.

Resilience to climate change and other shocks is increasingly a governance priority. Urban water systems must adapt to challenges such as droughts, floods, sea-level rise, and contamination events. This calls for policies that promote diversification of water sources, including rainwater harvesting, desalination, and wastewater reuse, alongside demand management measures. Contingency planning, risk assessments, and early-warning systems are vital components of adaptive governance.

Achieving inclusive and sustainable urban water systems also requires accountability and performance monitoring. Utilities and water authorities should be evaluated on service quality, equity of access, environmental performance, and financial management. Data transparency—through open dashboards, annual reports, and community engagement—supports informed decision-making and encourages continuous improvement.

Overall, governance for urban water systems is about balancing social equity, economic viability, and environmental stewardship. Cities that embed inclusivity and sustainability in their governance frameworks can ensure that water services remain reliable, resilient, and fair—serving both current and future generations while preserving the ecosystems on which they depend.

Chapter 8: Climate Resilience through Water Security (SDG 13)

Climate change is reshaping global water systems, altering precipitation patterns, intensifying extreme events, and affecting water quality. SDG 13 emphasizes the need for urgent climate action, with water security forming a cornerstone of resilience strategies. Droughts, floods, and shifting seasonal flows disrupt agriculture, energy production, urban water supply, and ecosystem health. Building resilience requires integrated approaches that combine grey infrastructure, such as reservoirs and flood defenses, with nature-based solutions like wetlands restoration and watershed management. Climate-smart governance ensures that water planning incorporates long-term risk assessments, adaptive management, and cross-sectoral coordination. Strengthening community-level adaptive capacity through early warning systems, demand management, and diversification of water sources reduces vulnerability to shocks. International cooperation on transboundary water systems and financing mechanisms for climate-resilient projects are essential to scale solutions. By placing water security at the heart of climate adaptation, societies can safeguard livelihoods, protect ecosystems, and support sustainable development.

Climate Change Impacts on Water Availability and Variability

Climate change is profoundly altering the hydrological cycle, reshaping patterns of water availability and introducing unprecedented variability in both timing and quantity of freshwater resources. Rising global temperatures accelerate the rate of evaporation from land and water surfaces, intensifying the water cycle and altering precipitation patterns. In many regions, this results in more extreme rainfall events interspersed with longer, more intense dry periods. The shifting climate disrupts traditional seasonal cycles that communities, agriculture, and industries have long relied upon, creating uncertainty in planning and resource allocation.

One of the most significant consequences of climate change on water resources is the changing distribution of precipitation. Some regions are experiencing increases in rainfall intensity, leading to floods, soil erosion, and sedimentation in rivers and reservoirs. Others are facing prolonged droughts, which reduce river flows, deplete groundwater reserves, and diminish the reliability of water supply systems. These shifts can occur within the same country or basin, exacerbating regional inequalities in access to water and challenging existing governance arrangements that were designed for more stable hydrological conditions.

Glacier and snowpack loss further compound the problem, especially in regions where meltwater is a critical component of annual river flow. As glaciers retreat and seasonal snowpack declines, water availability during dry months diminishes, placing stress on agriculture, hydropower generation, and urban supply. In coastal areas, sea-level rise contributes to saltwater intrusion into freshwater aquifers, reducing potable water availability and damaging agricultural land. The combined effect of these changes is a heightened risk of water scarcity, even in areas that historically enjoyed abundant supplies.

The variability introduced by climate change also increases the likelihood of conflict over water resources. Competition intensifies between sectors such as agriculture, industry, and municipal supply, particularly during periods of scarcity. Transboundary river basins face added complexities as upstream and downstream states navigate altered flow regimes. Traditional water management strategies—based on historical climate and hydrological data—are no longer adequate in the face of these dynamic changes. Instead, adaptive, forward-looking approaches that incorporate climate projections, flexible allocation mechanisms, and diversified supply options are becoming essential.

To address these challenges, integrated water resources management (IWRM) needs to be coupled with climate adaptation strategies that priorities resilience. This includes investment in infrastructure capable of handling greater variability, such as multipurpose reservoirs, improved irrigation systems, and enhanced flood defenses. Nature-based solutions, such as wetland restoration and reforestation, can also buffer against extremes by improving infiltration, regulating flows, and storing water in the landscape. Strengthening climate-informed governance, promoting regional cooperation, and ensuring that water allocation accounts for ecological as well as human needs will be critical to sustaining water security in a warming world.

Adapting Water Systems to Changing Extremes

As climate change intensifies the frequency and severity of extreme weather events, water systems must evolve to remain reliable and resilient. Floods, droughts, and heatwaves are placing unprecedented strain on infrastructure, operations, and governance. Traditional systems designed for historical climate conditions are increasingly inadequate, making adaptation a central priority for water managers, policymakers, and communities.

Flood events are becoming more intense due to heavier and more erratic rainfall patterns. Urban areas with impervious surfaces are especially vulnerable, as stormwater runoff can overwhelm drainage networks, leading to property damage, service interruptions, and public health risks. Upgrading stormwater systems, expanding green infrastructure, and restoring floodplains can help absorb and slow floodwaters, reducing peak flows into waterways. These measures also enhance water quality and biodiversity while providing recreational and cultural benefits.

Droughts, on the other hand, threaten both water supply and ecosystem health. Extended dry periods reduce river flows, deplete reservoirs, and strain groundwater reserves. To adapt, water systems must diversify their sources, incorporating options such as treated wastewater reuse, desalination, and managed aquifer recharge. Demand-side measures, including water efficiency standards, tiered pricing structures, and public education campaigns, can further alleviate pressure on limited supplies. Combining supply and demand strategies ensures greater resilience against prolonged shortages.

Temperature extremes also pose significant challenges, increasing evaporation from reservoirs and canals, elevating water demand for cooling, and impacting water quality through algal blooms and lower dissolved oxygen levels. Water treatment facilities may need technological upgrades to handle changing source water conditions, including higher sediment loads after storms or shifts in chemical composition during droughts. Proactive maintenance and adaptive operational protocols can help utilities respond swiftly to these evolving challenges.

Building resilience also involves embedding flexibility into planning and governance frameworks. Climate projections should be integrated into design standards for dams, levees, and pipelines to ensure they can handle a wider range of operating conditions. Real-time monitoring and data analytics can support more dynamic decision-making, enabling rapid adjustments in water allocation during crises. Cross-sector collaboration—linking water managers with energy, agriculture, and disaster risk reduction agencies—can strengthen preparedness and response capacity.

Community engagement is equally important. Local knowledge can help identify vulnerabilities and co-develop solutions that are culturally appropriate and socially inclusive. Public participation in planning builds trust and ensures that adaptation strategies address the needs of all groups, particularly those most at risk from climate extremes.

By investing in climate-resilient infrastructure, integrating natural systems into water management, and fostering adaptive governance, water systems can withstand the growing pressures of a changing climate. The ability to adjust to more frequent and severe extremes will be critical to safeguarding water security, protecting public health, and supporting economic stability in the decades ahead.

Nature-Based and Grey-Green Infrastructure Solutions

Nature-based and grey-green infrastructure solutions are increasingly recognized as essential approaches for addressing water management challenges in a changing climate. These solutions combine the strengths of natural ecosystems with engineered systems, offering flexible, adaptive, and cost-effective alternatives—or complements—to traditional grey infrastructure.

Nature-based solutions (NbS) harness processes such as filtration, storage, and flood regulation provided by forests, wetlands, grasslands, and river systems. They can be designed or restored to deliver specific water-related benefits, including improved water quality, enhanced groundwater recharge, and reduced flood risk. For example, wetland restoration upstream of urban areas can slow runoff, trap sediments, and filter pollutants before they enter rivers and reservoirs. Riparian buffers along waterways can stabilize banks, reduce erosion, and create habitats that strengthen biodiversity and ecological resilience.

Grey-green infrastructure integrates conventional built systems—such as pipes, culverts, and treatment plants—with green elements that mimic or enhance natural processes. Examples include permeable pavements that allow water to infiltrate into the ground, green roofs that retain rainwater and reduce peak flows, and bioswales that filter stormwater in urban streetscapes. This hybrid approach delivers multiple benefits: it reduces the burden on drainage and sewer networks, improves water quality, mitigates urban heat island effects, and provides accessible green spaces for communities.

An important advantage of grey-green solutions is their scalability. They can be implemented at small, decentralized scales—such as rain gardens in neighborhoods—or integrated into large-scale urban and regional water management strategies. Their modular nature allows for phased investment, enabling gradual transformation of urban and peri-urban landscapes without the large upfront costs associated with major infrastructure projects.

Economic resilience is also strengthened through these approaches. By reducing the need for extensive water treatment and flood damage repairs, nature-based and grey-green solutions often yield long-term cost savings. When combined with traditional grey systems, they enhance redundancy, meaning that if one component fails—such as during an extreme storm—others can continue functioning to protect communities and ecosystems.

However, successful implementation requires careful planning, cross-sector coordination, and supportive policy frameworks. Land-use planning must priorities space for natural systems, while water utilities, environmental agencies, and local governments collaborate to align goals and funding streams. Clear guidelines and standards can ensure that projects deliver measurable water management benefits alongside co-benefits such as carbon sequestration, recreation, and improved public health.

Monitoring and adaptive management are essential for ensuring that these systems continue to function effectively over time. Changes in climate, land use, and hydrological patterns may alter their performance, requiring adjustments in design or maintenance. Public engagement is also crucial, as communities play a key role in maintaining smaller-scale installations and advocating for their integration into local planning.

By blending the reliability of engineered systems with the adaptability and ecological benefits of natural processes, nature-based and grey-green infrastructure solutions represent a forward-looking strategy for water security. They offer pathways to manage water sustainably, enhance climate resilience, and create healthier, more livable environments.

Climate-Smart Water Governance and Planning

Climate-smart water governance and planning integrates climate resilience principles into the management of water resources, ensuring that policies, institutions, and decision-making processes are equipped to address both current challenges and future uncertainties. It recognizes that climate change is altering hydrological cycles, intensifying extremes, and shifting water availability patterns, requiring governance systems that are adaptive, inclusive, and forward-looking.

At its core, climate-smart governance involves embedding climate risk assessments into water policy development, infrastructure planning, and operational management. This means using climate projections alongside historical data to inform decisions on allocation, investment, and conservation. By planning for a range of possible future scenarios, water managers can better prepare for variability in supply, seasonal extremes, and long-term changes in demand.

Inclusive stakeholder engagement is a cornerstone of this approach. Water governance is most effective when it incorporates the perspectives and needs of all affected groups—governments, utilities, farmers, industries, communities, and marginalized populations. Participatory processes enhance legitimacy, promote transparency, and build trust, all of which are vital for implementing measures that may require behavioral and institutional changes. Integrating traditional and local knowledge with scientific expertise also strengthens decision-making by ensuring context-appropriate solutions.

Climate-smart planning emphasizes flexibility in infrastructure and policy frameworks. This includes adopting adaptive pathways, which allow for adjustments over time as new information emerges. For example, phased infrastructure upgrades can align with observed climate trends, avoiding the risk of overbuilding for scenarios that may not materialize. Similarly, regulatory frameworks can be designed to trigger changes in water allocation rules or drought restrictions based on pre-defined climate and hydrological thresholds.

Another critical element is mainstreaming water considerations across sectors. Climate-smart governance recognizes that water security is interconnected with energy, agriculture, urban development, and ecosystem management. Coordinated policies can prevent conflicts, enhance synergies, and maximize resource efficiency. For instance, integrating water planning with energy strategies can ensure that power generation does not compromise downstream water needs, while agricultural planning can priorities climate-resilient crops and irrigation systems that optimize water use.

Data, monitoring, and early warning systems form the backbone of climate-smart planning. Continuous tracking of hydrological indicators, combined with predictive modelling, enables proactive responses to floods, droughts, and other climate-related risks. Digital technologies, such as remote sensing and real-time data platforms, enhance situational awareness and facilitate rapid decision-making.

Financing mechanisms also need to evolve to support climate-smart approaches. Blending public funds, private investment, and climate finance can mobilize the resources necessary for innovation, infrastructure upgrades, and capacity building.

Through proactive, inclusive, and adaptive governance, climate-smart water planning enables societies to anticipate risks, seize opportunities, and safeguard water resources in an era of increasing climate uncertainty. This approach not only strengthens resilience but also supports sustainable development and long-term water security.

Enhancing Adaptive Capacity Through Integrated Water Risk Management

Enhancing adaptive capacity through integrated water risk management involves anticipating, reducing, and responding to the multiple risks that threaten water security, from scarcity and pollution to floods and infrastructure failures. This approach recognizes that risks are interconnected across hydrological, ecological, social, and economic systems, and therefore require coordinated responses that cut across sectors, governance levels, and timeframes.

At its foundation, integrated water risk management begins with comprehensive risk assessment. This means identifying vulnerabilities in water supply systems, ecosystems, and dependent livelihoods, while also mapping exposure to hazards such as droughts, floods, and contamination events. The assessment process should combine climate projections, hydrological modelling, and socio-economic analysis, enabling decision-makers to understand both the physical and human dimensions of water risks.

Once risks are identified, adaptive capacity is strengthened by embedding flexibility and redundancy into water systems. Flexible operational rules, such as dynamic allocation frameworks that adjust to seasonal conditions, allow systems to respond effectively to variability. Redundancy in supply sources—through measures such as diversifying water portfolios with rainwater harvesting, treated wastewater, and desalination—reduces dependence on any single source and increases resilience to shocks.

Integrated management also depends on breaking down silos between sectors. Water risk is closely tied to agriculture, energy, health, and urban planning, meaning that policies must align to avoid maladaptation. For example, agricultural subsidies can be redesigned to incentivize efficient irrigation and drought-tolerant crops, while urban planning regulations can incorporate green infrastructure to reduce flood risks. By linking water management with land use, disaster risk reduction, and environmental protection, governments can address root causes rather than symptoms.

Stakeholder engagement plays a critical role in adaptive capacity. Inclusive governance processes ensure that the perspectives of vulnerable groups—such as rural communities, women, and marginalized populations—are reflected in decision-making. This not only builds legitimacy and public trust but also draws on diverse knowledge systems, including local and indigenous practices that have evolved to manage variability.

Technology and data systems are central enablers of integrated risk management. Early warning systems, real-time monitoring networks, and predictive modelling can help anticipate hazards and guide proactive interventions. Combining these tools with contingency planning—such as pre-positioning emergency water supplies or establishing rapid-response teams—can reduce both economic losses and human suffering during crises.

Financing strategies must support the entire risk management cycle, from prevention and preparedness to response and recovery. Leveraging climate finance, insurance mechanisms, and public–private partnerships can provide the resources needed to sustain long-term adaptation measures.

By integrating these elements, water risk management becomes not just a defensive strategy but a driver of resilience, enabling communities, economies, and ecosystems to adapt to uncertainty while safeguarding development gains.

Chapter 9: Strengthening Global Partnerships and Governance (SDG 17)

Achieving water security in line with the SDGs requires strong global partnerships and robust governance mechanisms. SDG 17 underscores the importance of collaboration across governments, international organizations, civil society, and the private sector to mobilize resources, share knowledge, and align policies. Effective governance frameworks enable coherent and integrated approaches, linking water management to poverty reduction, health, climate resilience, and economic growth. Partnerships are vital for facilitating technology transfer, improving data sharing and monitoring systems, and building institutional capacity, particularly in developing countries. Public-private and multistakeholder initiatives can drive innovation, mobilize investment, and ensure that solutions are inclusive and equitable. Strengthening institutions at all levels fosters accountability, transparency, and coordination between sectors and jurisdictions. Through cooperative action, shared responsibility, and sustained investment, global partnerships and governance can accelerate progress towards universal water security, ensuring that no community or ecosystem is left behind in the pursuit of the SDG agenda.

International Cooperation on Transboundary Water Issues

International cooperation on transboundary water issues is essential for ensuring equitable, sustainable, and peaceful management of shared water resources. With over 260 river basins and countless aquifers crossing political boundaries, many of the world's most vital freshwater systems are shared by two or more countries. These shared waters sustain agriculture, energy production, biodiversity, and livelihoods, making their governance central to regional stability and development.

The complexity of managing transboundary waters arises from the fact that upstream and downstream countries often have different priorities, economic capacities, and political interests. Upstream states may focus on hydropower development or irrigation expansion, while downstream states priorities secure flows for agriculture, drinking water, or navigation. These differing needs can create tensions, especially during periods of scarcity or in the context of climate change, which is altering the timing and quantity of river flows. Effective cooperation helps to prevent disputes and transform potential conflicts into opportunities for joint benefit.

At the heart of cooperation is the principle of equitable and reasonable utilization, a core tenet of international water law enshrined in instruments such as the 1997 UN Convention on the Law of the Non-Navigational Uses of International Watercourses. This principle balances the rights and obligations of riparian states, ensuring that no country's use of a shared resource causes significant harm to others. Complementing this is the duty to cooperate, which requires countries to share data, consult on planned measures, and establish mechanisms for joint decision-making.

Basin-level agreements are the most effective means of operationalizing these principles. Successful examples include treaties that establish joint river commissions or basin authorities with mandates for monitoring, planning, and dispute resolution. These bodies can coordinate infrastructure development, harmonies water quality standards, and set allocation rules that adapt to changing conditions. In groundwater systems, where boundaries are less visible and data is often sparse, agreements can promote joint mapping, monitoring, and recharge projects to ensure long-term sustainability.

Data and information sharing are critical for building trust and enabling informed decision-making. Regular exchanges of hydrological data, water quality measurements, and climate projections help countries anticipate changes and plan accordingly. Joint scientific studies and shared modelling platforms can provide a common evidence base, reducing the likelihood of disputes over facts. Advances in remote sensing and open-access satellite imagery have further expanded opportunities for transparent monitoring, even in politically sensitive contexts.

Economic and environmental cooperation can strengthen transboundary water governance by creating incentives for collaboration. Joint investments in infrastructure—such as multipurpose dams, navigation channels, or flood protection systems—can deliver shared economic benefits. Environmental cooperation, such as coordinated wetland restoration or pollution control measures, can improve ecosystem health across borders, benefiting communities and biodiversity alike. Such initiatives are often more successful when linked to broader regional integration efforts, where water becomes part of a wider agenda of trade, energy, and transport cooperation.

International organizations, development banks, and regional bodies play an important role in facilitating cooperation. They can provide neutral platforms for dialogue, technical expertise, and financing for joint projects. In some cases, third-party mediation or arbitration may be needed to resolve disputes, particularly in politically sensitive basins. Capacity-building programs can also help riparian countries develop the technical and institutional skills needed to engage effectively in negotiations and implement agreements.

Climate change underscores the urgency of cooperation on transboundary water issues. Changing precipitation patterns, glacier melt, and increased droughts and floods are amplifying uncertainties in water availability, making unilateral actions riskier. Adaptive, flexible agreements that incorporate climate projections and allow for periodic review are better equipped to deal with these challenges.

Through sustained dialogue, transparent data sharing, and joint action, countries can turn shared water resources into platforms for peace, prosperity, and resilience. International cooperation not only reduces the risk of conflict but also enhances the collective ability of states to manage water in a way that supports sustainable development and climate adaptation.

Financing Mechanisms for SDG-Aligned Water Projects

Achieving the SDGs for water—particularly SDG 6 on clean water and sanitation—requires substantial investment in infrastructure, technology, and governance systems. These investments must be both financially viable and socially inclusive, ensuring access for all while safeguarding environmental resources. Mobilising adequate and well-targeted finance is a central challenge, as water projects often require large upfront capital, long payback periods, and involve public goods that generate limited direct revenue. A diverse set of financing mechanisms has emerged to address these challenges, each offering different opportunities for aligning projects with SDG objectives.

Public financing remains a cornerstone of SDG-aligned water initiatives. Governments often provide funding through budget allocations, grants, or concessional loans, especially for projects that deliver essential services to underserved populations. Public funds are critical for building and maintaining infrastructure such as water supply networks, wastewater treatment plants, and rural water systems, which may not attract sufficient private investment. Many governments also leverage official development assistance (ODA) from bilateral and multilateral donors, targeting interventions that close access gaps, improve quality, and enhance resilience.

Private sector participation is increasingly recognized as vital for scaling up investment. Public–private partnerships (PPPs) allow governments to share risks and responsibilities with private operators while benefiting from private capital, expertise, and innovation. Under well-designed contracts, private partners can finance, build, and operate infrastructure, with payment mechanisms tied to service performance. For projects to remain SDG-aligned, PPP frameworks must incorporate affordability safeguards, transparency requirements, and measurable sustainability outcomes.

Blended finance has become a key tool for bridging the gap between public and private sources. By using concessional public or philanthropic funds to reduce the perceived risks for commercial investors, blended finance can catalyze private capital flows into projects that might otherwise be considered too risky. This can take the form of first-loss guarantees, interest rate subsidies, or co-financing arrangements. Such mechanisms are particularly effective in emerging markets, where credit risks and regulatory uncertainties can deter private investment.

Innovative financing instruments are also gaining traction. Green bonds and sustainability-linked loans enable investors to support projects with clear environmental and social benefits, including water conservation, wastewater treatment, and flood resilience. Debt-for-nature or debt-for-water swaps allow indebted countries to redirect debt servicing payments into water-related environmental projects. Impact investment funds, which target both financial returns and measurable development outcomes, are another channel for mobilizing resources toward SDG-compliant water initiatives.

Tariff reforms and cost recovery policies, when implemented equitably, can enhance the financial sustainability of water service providers, making them more creditworthy and better able to attract investment. However, such reforms must be accompanied by targeted subsidies or lifeline tariffs to protect low-income households from affordability constraints.

International climate finance offers another important avenue, especially as climate change increasingly affects water security. Funds such as the Green Climate Fund (GCF) and Adaptation Fund provide grants and concessional finance for projects that integrate climate resilience into water management, from drought-resistant supply systems to flood protection infrastructure.

Effective financing for SDG-aligned water projects requires a coordinated approach that blends multiple sources and instruments, links investment decisions to clear sustainability criteria, and ensures that financial mechanisms deliver equitable access, environmental protection, and long-term resilience. By combining public commitment, private innovation, and targeted international support, countries can mobilize the scale of investment needed to meet water-related SDGs.

Data Sharing, Monitoring, and Capacity Development

Robust data sharing, effective monitoring, and strong capacity development are fundamental pillars for achieving water-related SDGs. Water systems are complex, interconnected, and subject to rapid changes driven by climate variability, demographic pressures, and evolving economic activities. Without accurate, timely, and accessible data, decision-makers face significant challenges in planning, managing, and adapting water resources sustainably. Integrating these three elements—data sharing, monitoring, and capacity development—ensures that policies and investments are evidence-based, inclusive, and adaptive.

Data sharing fosters collaboration across institutions, sectors, and borders. Water resources do not conform to administrative boundaries, making cooperation between different jurisdictions essential. Transparent sharing of hydrological, meteorological, and water quality data enables coordinated management of rivers, aquifers, and other shared resources. Open data platforms, supported by standardized collection methods and metadata protocols, allow researchers, policymakers, utilities, and communities to work from a common information base. This transparency not only improves trust between stakeholders but also reduces duplication of effort, speeds up crisis response, and supports integrated water resource management.

Monitoring systems provide the foundation for understanding the state of water resources and the performance of interventions.

Effective monitoring goes beyond measuring availability and quality—it tracks infrastructure functionality, service delivery, demand trends, and the effectiveness of policies. Technological innovations such as remote sensing, satellite imagery, IoT-enabled sensors, and automated data loggers have significantly expanded the capacity to monitor in real time and at scale. However, sustained investment in ground-based monitoring stations and laboratory facilities remains essential to verify and complement remotely sensed data. Reliable monitoring frameworks should align with internationally recognized SDG indicators, enabling comparability and progress tracking at both national and global levels.

Capacity development is critical to ensure that data and monitoring systems are used effectively. Even the most advanced tools and datasets cannot improve water governance without skilled personnel who can interpret, analyze, and apply information in decision-making. Capacity development involves training technical staff in data collection, analysis, and modelling, as well as strengthening institutional capabilities for planning, enforcement, and stakeholder engagement. It also includes fostering leadership and communication skills among water managers, enabling them to convey complex information to policymakers and the public in a way that informs action.

The integration of data sharing, monitoring, and capacity development requires coordinated institutional frameworks. Governments can lead by establishing clear mandates for data management, setting standards for quality control, and incentivizing inter-agency and cross-border collaboration. Partnerships with academic institutions, civil society, and the private sector can further strengthen technical expertise and innovation.

In addition, aligning these efforts with digital transformation strategies can maximize efficiency. Cloud-based data repositories, open-source software tools, and mobile applications can lower barriers to access and facilitate stakeholder participation, especially in low-resource settings. Investments in cybersecurity and data governance ensure that sensitive information is protected while maintaining transparency.

By embedding data sharing, monitoring, and capacity development into water sector strategies, countries can create a knowledge-driven foundation for achieving water-related SDGs, improving resilience, and ensuring equitable and sustainable access to water resources for all.

Public-Private and Multistakeholder Partnerships

Public-private and multistakeholder partnerships are essential mechanisms for mobilizing resources, expertise, and innovation to achieve water-related SDGs. Water challenges are inherently cross-cutting, involving government agencies, businesses, civil society, and communities. No single actor can address these complexities alone, making collaboration across sectors vital for sustainable and equitable water management.

Public-private partnerships (PPPs) leverage the strengths of both sectors. Governments provide regulatory frameworks, long-term vision, and public accountability, while private entities contribute capital investment, technical know-how, and operational efficiency. In the water sector, PPPs can support infrastructure development, such as treatment plants, distribution networks, and wastewater facilities, by combining public oversight with private sector project delivery capabilities. They can also accelerate the adoption of innovative technologies, including desalination systems, smart metering, and advanced water treatment methods. Well-designed PPP contracts should balance commercial viability with public service obligations, ensuring affordability, service quality, and environmental safeguards.

Beyond traditional PPPs, multistakeholder partnerships broaden the collaborative landscape to include non-governmental organizations (NGOs), academia, community-based groups, and international development agencies. These partnerships create platforms where diverse perspectives and priorities can be reconciled, enabling more inclusive decision-making. In many contexts, multistakeholder forums help mediate between competing demands—such as agriculture, industry, and environmental protection—by fostering dialogue and trust-building. They also promote knowledge exchange, allowing innovations tested in one context to be adapted and scaled in others.

The success of these partnerships depends on clear governance structures. Defined roles, transparent decision-making processes, and equitable distribution of benefits are critical to sustaining engagement over time. Monitoring and evaluation frameworks should be built into partnership agreements to track progress, assess impacts, and make necessary adjustments. Regular reporting enhances accountability, helping stakeholders maintain confidence in the process.

Financing is a central element of both PPPs and multistakeholder initiatives. Blended finance approaches—combining public funds, private investment, and donor contributions—can de-risk projects and attract capital for initiatives that might otherwise be considered too risky or low-return. Development banks, climate finance mechanisms, and philanthropic organizations can provide concessional financing or guarantees to catalyze private sector involvement in water projects aligned with SDG targets.

Capacity building within partnerships ensures that all actors can participate effectively. Governments may require support in contract negotiation and project oversight, while communities may need training in water management practices to sustain benefits over the long term. Similarly, private sector actors benefit from understanding local social and environmental contexts, enabling them to design solutions that are both technically sound and socially accepted.

By fostering collaboration across public, private, and societal spheres, these partnerships create a shared platform for aligning investment, innovation, and policy. This alignment enhances the resilience, efficiency, and inclusivity of water systems, helping to accelerate progress towards the SDGs while ensuring that no one is left behind.

Strengthening Institutions for Integrated SDG Delivery

Strengthening institutions is central to achieving integrated delivery of the SDGs, particularly in the water sector where multiple goals intersect. Effective institutions provide the governance architecture, coordination mechanisms, and policy coherence required to manage water as a cross-cutting resource that underpins health, food security, energy production, and ecosystem integrity. Without strong institutional capacity, SDG implementation risks becoming fragmented, with overlapping mandates, inefficient resource allocation, and inconsistent policy execution.

An integrated approach begins with aligning institutional mandates across sectors and administrative levels. Many countries have separate agencies responsible for water supply, sanitation, agriculture, energy, and environment, often operating with limited communication or joint planning. Strengthening institutions means creating or enhancing coordination platforms that bring together these agencies to develop coherent strategies, share data, and synchronize investment plans. Legislative frameworks can be updated to embed integrated water management principles, ensuring that all relevant sectors operate under common sustainability objectives.

Capacity development within institutions is equally important. Technical expertise, policy analysis skills, and the ability to apply systems thinking are critical for navigating the interdependencies of the SDGs. Training programs, knowledge exchanges, and partnerships with universities or research institutions can help build this capacity. Strengthening human resources also involves retaining skilled staff through incentives, professional development opportunities, and clear career pathways.

Institutions must also embrace adaptive governance to respond to dynamic challenges such as climate change, population growth, and shifting economic priorities. This involves building flexibility into policies and operational plans, enabling rapid adjustments when conditions change. Scenario planning, risk assessments, and monitoring systems support informed decision-making and help institutions anticipate and mitigate emerging threats.

Transparency and accountability are essential for sustaining public trust and ensuring that integrated SDG delivery benefits all segments of society. Open data portals, participatory planning processes, and regular public reporting create opportunities for citizens, civil society organizations, and the private sector to contribute to and monitor progress. This not only improves legitimacy but also fosters innovation by allowing external actors to identify and address gaps.

Financial stability underpins institutional effectiveness. Securing adequate, predictable funding—whether through public budgets, donor support, or innovative financing mechanisms—enables institutions to plan long-term projects and maintain essential services. Resource allocation processes should priorities projects that deliver co-benefits across multiple SDGs, ensuring efficient use of funds.

By aligning mandates, building capacity, fostering adaptability, promoting transparency, and securing sustainable financing, strengthened institutions can act as the backbone for integrated SDG delivery. Such institutions are better equipped to coordinate across sectors, mobilize diverse actors, and translate global commitments into locally relevant, inclusive, and resilient outcomes.

Conclusion

Achieving water security within the framework of the SDGs requires a holistic, integrated approach that recognizes water as both a standalone priority and a cross-cutting enabler of progress across multiple sectors. Water underpins human health, food production, energy generation, economic development, and environmental sustainability. Its effective management is therefore essential not only for SDG 6 but also for the broader 2030 Agenda, including goals on poverty eradication, gender equality, climate action, and sustainable cities.

Throughout the analysis, it becomes clear that progress in water security demands coordinated action across governance, finance, technology, and social inclusion. Strong institutional frameworks are necessary to ensure coherence across policy domains, aligning mandates, reducing duplication, and fostering collaboration between different levels of government and sectors. Building institutional capacity—through skills development, adequate resources, and adaptive governance systems—enables actors to respond effectively to both persistent challenges and emerging risks, from climate extremes to demographic shifts.

Water security also depends on equitable access, ensuring that all communities—particularly vulnerable and marginalized groups—can rely on safe, affordable, and reliable water and sanitation services. Equity considerations must be embedded in water-related planning and investment decisions, not as an afterthought but as a guiding principle. This extends to recognising the disproportionate burden on women and girls in water collection, ensuring gender-responsive policies, and promoting inclusive participation in water governance.

The integration of technological solutions, nature-based approaches, and infrastructure investments forms a cornerstone of sustainable water management. Advanced monitoring systems, wastewater reuse, and energy-efficient water treatment technologies can improve efficiency and resilience, while green and grey-green infrastructure can address challenges such as flooding, drought, and pollution. However, these innovations must be supported by enabling policies, targeted financing, and capacity building to ensure they are scalable and accessible across contexts.

Financing remains a decisive factor in the success of water-related SDG implementation. Public investment, private sector engagement, and blended finance mechanisms all play a role in mobilizing the resources needed to close infrastructure gaps, maintain services, and address environmental externalities. Linking investment decisions to SDG outcomes ensures that financial flows support projects with broad societal benefits, including co-benefits across health, climate, and economic productivity.

International and regional cooperation is equally vital, especially for transboundary water resources. Sharing data, harmonizing standards, and coordinating management strategies can prevent conflict, promote equitable allocation, and enhance resilience in shared basins. Partnerships between governments, civil society, research institutions, and the private sector enable the pooling of expertise and resources, amplifying the impact of interventions.

The path to achieving water security is both complex and urgent. It requires sustained political will, innovative thinking, and a commitment to inclusivity. By strengthening institutions, aligning policies, integrating equity, leveraging technology, and securing adequate financing, it is possible to make tangible progress toward water-related SDGs. This integrated approach not only safeguards water resources but also accelerates broader sustainable development, ensuring that the benefits of water security are realized for present and future generations.

www.ingramcontent.com/pod-product-compliance
Lightning Source LLC
Chambersburg PA
CBHW050531240926
51846CB00003B/774